MW00718475

Jeff's devotional
uplifting. In life
of devotionals tha.
profound deeper truths of God and His Word.

—BOBBY THOMPSON
District Superintendent
West Florida District Council of the Assemblies of God

Jeff Scalf's devotionals are truly inspiring! Jeff's own rich, personal relationship with Jesus comes through in each entry. It's easy to see he's "been with Jesus," for his writings carry that presence—fresh, encouraging, and honest. They feed my heart, and I know they'll feed all who open these pages!

—PHIL EDWARDS
Assistant District Superintendent
West Florida District Council of the Assemblies of God

A wise homiletics professor once instructed; "Gentlemen, exercise the grace of conciseness!" The deep truths of life are not always discovered in the many volumes of books that line a pastors' shelf. Rather, they are discovered in the simple statements and stories from another person's heart. Pastor Jeff has accomplished the grace of conciseness while challenging the hearts of all believers as well as pastors. His devotional writing is fresh, crisp, and to the point. With so much that begs for believers' and ministers' time and focus, it is a joy to be captured by the insights of a comrade's heart. Pastor Jeff speaks from the heart to the heart of his peers and all believers and for that we are all better servants.

—DR GARRY L. BRACKETT
Senior Pastor
Callaway Assembly of God
Panama City, Florida

COLLECTIONS FOR THE

JOURNEY
of life

COLLECTIONS FOR THE

JOURNEY

of life

JEFF SCALF

TATE PUBLISHING & *Enterprises*

Published by Tate Publishing & Enterprises, LLC
127 E. Trade Center Terrace | Mustang, Oklahoma 73064 USA
1.888.361.9473 | www.tatepublishing.com

Tate Publishing is committed to excellence in the publishing industry. The company reflects the philosophy established by the founders, based on Psalm 68:11,
"The Lord gave the word and great was the company of those who published it."

Book design copyright © 2008 by Tate Publishing, LLC. All rights reserved.
Cover design by Kandi Evans
Interior design by Kellie Southerland

Published in the United States of America

ISBN: 978-1-60604-946-4
1. Christian Living: Practical Life: General
2. General Interest: Motivational: Devotionals
08.08.06

DEDICATION

I dedicate this first book to my mother, Barbara Scalf, whose faith and example have molded the faith that I have obtained. In my younger days of ministry, she would always tell me before I preached, "make sure you're not preaching from the book of Jeffery." Well this is the book of "Jeffery" but the book of "Jeffery" is all based on the Word of God. Thanks mom for your faith and love.

I acknowledge my wife Shawn, who encouraged me more than once to publish some of my devotionals. The Bible says, "He who finds a wife finds a good thing, and obtains favor from the LORD" Pro 18:22 (NJKV). I have truly found a good thing and have obtained favor from the LORD. I would also like to acknowledge my two wonderful children who are such a joy to me. My daughter, Breanna, whom I hope will one day be an accomplished Christian author in her own right and my son, Josiah, who I pray will follow the steps of Christ in whatever calling He leads.

COLLECTIONS

INTRODUCTION

Collections ~ For the Journey of Life is a collection of devotionals I have written from my personal experiences, observations and from my time in the Word with Jesus. They are to be a supplement to your personal devotions. My goal for these writings is to inspire, challenge, and make Christians stop to ponder upon the greater wonders and deeper truths of God's Word. I pray that God will use them to be a blessing and draw you closer to Him.

THE OLD MAN
AT THE MOUNTAIN

PROV 12:1; PROV 2:1–15; 3:1–3; 4:1–2

LIFE'S JOURNEY

Two teenagers, Tom and Grant, were traveling down the road of life and they came to a mountain range. There was no way around it; they had to go through the rough terrain to get where they were going in life. At the foot of this mountain range, there was an old man. This old man had an old road map in his hand. One of the teens, Grant, walked over to ask the old man for directions.

OLD MAP

The old man said, "Here son, take this road map, for it has served me well while traversing these rugged mountains. I have clearly marked the map of all the hazards and marked the path that although harder, will be safer. Now when you come to the ..."

"Oh come on Grant...we don't need that old man's advice...I can lead us through with no problem," exclaimed Tom.

"I see you've already been this way before," said the old man to Tom.

"Well, no I haven't, but I'm smart enough to make it through this mountain range without the advice of some old man like you. Taking your way is slow and boring, I plan on taking this mountain with all the gusto and adventure I can."

"So you foresee no danger or hazard of death along this rugged terrain," asked the old man. "You know, there have been a number of teenagers, like yourself, that have been seriously hurt, maimed, or killed because they took the wrong turn along these mountain paths," he continued.

"So I suppose an old man like you with an old worn map can tell us the right way...besides what makes you the expert anyway," Tom said with a snide attitude.

THE DIPLOMA OF HARD KNOCKS

With that, the old man pulled up his left shirtsleeve to expose a nasty looking scar.

"What, a scar from stumbling as an old man?" Tom said mockingly.

Then the old man pulled up his left paints leg to reveal another nasty scar.

"Ok, so it was a big fall from tripping over your old age, what's that got to do with making you an expert?" rebuffed Tom.

Then old man lifted up his shirt to mid chest and his left side was riddled with scars and indentations in his flesh where obviously, there had been tremendous trauma.

"Where did you get those scars?" said Grant with silent amazement.

A Story of Regret

"Many years ago," stated the old man, "I was a teenager traveling this same road as you. It was at this very spot that I too met an old man such as myself today. He too offered me a road map that would show me the way to safely navigate through this rugged mountain terrain. However, I was arrogant and stupid and would not listen to his advice. My friend traveling with me wanted to heed the old man's advice but I persuaded him otherwise. Reluctantly my friend followed me."

"I had never been through this mountain range before so had not a clue of the dangers that awaited me. We came to a pass that was but a twelve-inch ledge against the face of the mountain to cross to the continuing path. I put my friend in front and coaxed him to go. Halfway through, the ledge gave way and he and I fell to the unknown below. I landed on a jagged ledge about 40 feet below. My friend however, continued another 200 feet to his death.

I closed my eyes, sure that death was near, for my body was twisted and racked in pain. A few hours later, I awoke by a fire and felt warm oil being poured into my wounds. I looked up to see the old man that had warned me at the bottom of the mountain. It took months for me to recover and then I continued on my journey, but this time with the old man's map in hand. The map was true it did not lead me wrong, but warned of me all the dangers and plotted for me a safe path."

"So my two young friends, a choice you must make. Press on, on your own and face the dangers unknown or take my map to guide you through to the other side. For I have been through this way before and wished I had listened to the old man before."

What Would Be Your Choice?

So if you were Grant who would you listen to, a friend that has never trekked the path before or an old man that has been there and knows the dangers before you?

I told my daughter a similar story when she became a teenager. I asked her who would you listen to, your friend, who has never been that way before or the old man. She said the old man. I asked her why and she replied, "Because the old man has been there before and knows where all the danger is."

Who is The Old Man?

I told her that in this story, I am the old man and she is the teenager who has never been that way before.

I said, "you're going have some choices to make as you go through these teenage years, you can listen to the old man or you can listen to your friends. However, I can assure you that the old man has a few scars from not listening to his old man when he was going through his teenage years."

> "My son, do not forget my law, But let your heart keep my commands; For length of days and long life And peace they will add to you."
>
> Prov 3:1–2 (NKJV)

THE JOURNEY HOME–PART 1
LUKE 15:11–24

RUDE AWAKENING

He was awakened by the strong, foul smell of rotting food mixed with sour mud. His face grimaced from the intense hunger pains since he hadn't eaten in days. As he got up from the mud that he had slept in, a thought raced through his mind, *my father's servants live like kings compared to this.* His mind raced to how he used to live in relative ease when he lived at home. The pain of sorrow, shame, and regret also began to rise to the forefront.

A tear left his eye and made a muddy streak down his face as he thought about his father. The callousness of rebellion was now gone and the realization of what a fool he had been now glared at him. When he packed his bags and left, he couldn't wait to get out from under all the father's rules! He couldn't wait to do what he wanted to do. He couldn't wait to live the life he wanted to live.

More Tears

More tears of pain and sorrow rolled down his face as his mind raced even further back to his childhood. He remembered the warm embraces of his father. He remembered the times that his father would take him on hunting and fishing excursions and the stories that he would tell around the dinner table.

However, the thought that brought the most tears yet was the remembrance of his father's words "son, I love you." Tears turned to weeping as he remembered that those were the last words he heard his father say the day he stormed out of the house in utter detest for his father.

A Most Pitiful Sight

Here was indeed a most pitiful sight one could behold, a wayward son weeping in the middle of a pigpen. He had come to a point lower than he could have ever imagined being in. Perhaps, just perhaps, he could return to his father and confess that he has sinned against him and against heaven and that he was not worthy or expected to be called his son anymore. If he would be merciful he would allow him to be a servant; at least the servants had food, clothing, and shelter.

A Journey Begins with the First Step

He climbed out of the pigpen, got his wits about him, and started in the direction of his father's house. He knew that he was several days journey from his father's house so he had some time to think. Unbeknownst to him, this journey home would not be as easy as he had thought it would be.

〜

Over the next few devotionals, we are going to journey with this prodigal as he takes his journey home. Perhaps you or someone you know is a "prodigal." This is one that used to have a relationship with Christ but has walked away and is now living in sin.

Today, we see that the first step for a wayward son to come back to God is that they must come to themselves and acknowledge they are away from God and living in the pigpen of sin. Unless they come to this point, they will never see the need to take the journey home. If you have friends and/or loved ones that are prodigals, the most important prayer you can pray is that they will come to themselves. If you are a prodigal, do you realize the state you are in? Do you realize that you are in the pigpen of sin?

> For godly sorrow produces repentance leading to salvation, not to be regretted; but the sorrow of the world produces death.
>
> 2 Cor 7:10 (NKJV)

> If we confess our sins, He is faithful and just to forgive us our sins and to cleanse us from all unrighteousness.
>
> 1 John 1:9 (NKJV)

If you are a prodigal start your journey home today!

THE JOURNEY HOME–PART 2
LUKE 15:11–24

His once fine clothes were now torn, stained, and tattered. He hadn't had a bath in over a month, and he hadn't eaten in days. He was a prodigal on the road home to beg his father to just allow him to be one of his servants. Although he was several days from home, he thought it would be relatively easy to make it there. However, as he would soon find out it would not be as easy as he thought.

OLD FAMILIAR PLACE

As he journeyed the road, it took him past some recently familiar sights in the town in which he had lived his riotous life. The first person he met along the road was Livea. She was a beautiful woman that he had spent a many a night with in his party days.

"Prod, is that you?" she said. "What happened to you!?"

"You remember! I ran out of money," Prod said in a tone mixed with shame and anger.

"Oh, that's right," she responded in a thoughtful tone.

"No one would let me live with them, so I had to live in a pigpen, but now I'm on a journey home," said Prod.

"Prod, you know you cannot live without me," she said as she walked towards him with a seductive smile upon her face. "I know you haven't forgotten all the good times we've had?" The closer she came to Prod she got a whiff of the pigpen and grimaced and took a step back to gain her composure.

"We can have even more good times. In fact, there's a new guy in town and he's loaded with money and looking for friends. Go down to the river, wash up, and meet me here tonight and we'll be his friends and have some good times again. You know you cannot live without me."

With that, she blew him a seductive kiss and walked way. Oh how he remembered those "good times."

SEEING HIMSELF IN ANOTHER

As he stood there contemplating if he could live without Livea, he saw a group of people following a young man. This young man was dressed in fine apparel and was boasting of how much money he had to those who were clamoring around him. As he watched them pass by, he realized that was him not too long ago. He remembered all the "friends" he had when he had money to burn and how all those "friends" forsook him when he went broke. Why even Livea forsook him when he went broke.

No! I can live without Livea. She's not my friend. She's the one that I spent most of my money on to begin with, and the first one to dump me when I ran out of money. With friends like her, who needs enemies, he thought.

THE JOURNEY IS NOT AS EASY AS FIRST THOUGHT

When a prodigal comes to himself and realizes how far he's strayed from God, he is going to face several people along the journey home that will try to convince him not to return to God. Usually one of the first people is "Livea" in that you cannot "live ah without me or it."

You cannot live without the alcohol. You cannot live without pornography. You cannot live without the drugs. You cannot live without the "party crowd." You cannot live without that illicit relationship. You cannot live without whatever sent you to the pigpen in the first place.

The devil blinds the prodigals to the truth.

> And no wonder! For Satan himself transforms himself into an angel of light.
>
> 2 Cor 11:14 (NKJV)

> But even if our gospel is veiled, it is veiled to those who are perishing, ⁴whose minds the god of this age has blinded, who do not believe, lest the light of the gospel of the glory of Christ, who is the image of God, should shine on them.
>
> 2 Cor 4:3–4 (NKJV)

CAN HE LIVE-AH WITHOUT IT?

The prodigal knows he's away from home but doesn't think he can live without the sin that sent him to the pigpen in the first place. If you know a prodigal who knows they are away from God, pray that the Holy Spirit will remove the blinders from their spiritual eyes to see the truth. The truth is that they can live without it and that Livea is what sent them to the pigpen.

If you are a prodigal and you know you're away from God but don't believe you can live without "Livea," realize it's all a lie from the devil. Livea is only interested in keeping you in the pigpen. She may party with you, but when the party is over, she'll dump you back into the pigpen.

As we continue our journey home with the prodigal, we will see that he will continue to meet those who will try to convince him not to journey back home.

THE JOURNEY HOME–PART 3
LUKE 15:11–24

PRESSING ON IN THE JOURNEY

The prodigal pressed his way on in his journey home. He had just left Livea, realizing that she was no good for him. His thoughts now once again returned to his father and the life he once had while living at home. A few miles outside the city that he had spent his riotous life in, he met two brothers, Liar and Condemnation.

Prod had seen these guys around town many times but had never talked with them.

"Hey Prod," one of them said. "Where are you going"?

"I've made a mess of my life, and I'm going back home to my father to beg him to just let me be a servant. At least I will have a place to live and food to eat."

CONDEMNATION SPOKE UP

"Do you really think that your father is going to forgive you? You took your inheritance before your father died, which is taboo. You turned your back on him in absolute defiance of his rules. You've wasted your inheritance on harlots and drunkenness and now you want him to take you back? If you were him, would you take you back?"

LIAR CHIMED IN

"Your father won't take you back. To him you're as good as dead, and he's forgotten all about you. If he sees you again, he'll spit in your face and tell you that you've gotten what you deserve. You'll never be accepted by him ever again. You know the cultural norms. When you took your inheritance before your father died and then walked away from him, you were no longer a part of his family. Therefore, you have no right to go back and beg for forgiveness."

Condemnation spoke again, "You're just going to have to live with this the rest of your life. You're going to have to live like this the rest of your life. You're going to have live with your regrets forever till the day you die."

COULD IT BE?

The prodigal hung his head in shame and defeat. "Could it be? Are they right?" The thoughts of his defiance, the thoughts of the foolish squandering of his inheritance and life, the thoughts of the cultural norms and the fact that it was customary for a father to cut off a child from the family if he rebelled.

OCEAN OF DESPAIR AND WAVES OF REGRET

He fell to his knees and began to weep. He was sinking in an ocean of despair. The waves of regrets washed over him drowning him with remorse. However, in the midst of this a thought from his childhood beamed through the clouds of this emotional storm. He remembered when he was a child and had fell out of a tree his father had warned him not to climb. He was hurt and crying and his father ran to him and picked him up in his arms and said, "It's ok son, I'm here." His father didn't scold him or tell him "I told you…" He simply held him close and said, "I love you, son."

THE LIFE RAFT IN THE OCEAN OF DESPAIR

The prodigal began to remember that "I love you, son" was spoken quite often to him all throughout his life, when he was obedient and when he was being disciplined. Could the father still love him even after all he'd done? Not once throughout his entire life, did the father ever say, "I hate you." Not once did the father respond with malice in the face of his son's defiance. Not once, not even in the midst of punishment did his father show anything but love and concern for what was best for his son.

The prodigal got up and pressed on with his journey back home. He was willing to take a chance that his father may not forgive him. He was willing to take a chance that his father would reject him. He was willing to take any punishment the father deemed just.

THEY WILL CONFRONT YOU!

Those who are prodigals on the journey home will face Liar and Condemnation. If you know a prodigal, pray that they will see God the Father as one who will forgive those who are truly repentant and sorrowful for their sins. Pray that the Holy Spirit of truth will speak through the cloud of doubt that Liar and Condemnation has spoken to them.

If you are a prodigal and you think that you've gone too far for God to forgive, you're wrong. The fact that you feel any regret whatsoever is proof you've not gone too far for God to forgive. Don't allow Liar and Condemnation to stop you from pressing on to the Father.

> For godly sorrow produces repentance leading to salvation, not to be regretted; but the sorrow of the world produces death.

2 Cor 7:10 (NKJV)

If we confess our sins, He is faithful and just to forgive us our sins and to cleanse us from all unrighteousness.

1 John 1:9 (NKJV)

For God so loved the world that He gave His only begotten Son, that whoever believes in Him should not perish but have everlasting life.

John 3:16 (NKJV)

"Come now, and let us reason together," says the LORD, "Though your sins are like scarlet, they shall be as white as snow; though they are red like crimson, they shall be as wool.

Isa 1:18 (NKJV)

THE JOURNEY HOME–PART 4
LUKE 15:11–24

The prodigal had passed by Livea, Liar, and Condemnation, three persuasive people that tried to convince him not to journey back home. He had made good progress and was just a couple of hours away from arriving at his father's house. As he stopped along the way to rest under a shade tree another traveler stopped to rest as well.

DISCOURAGEMENT

The fellow traveler introduced himself as Discouragement. As the two began to strike up a conversation, the conversation lead to the prodigal telling his story and of his journey home.

"You know," said Discouragement, "you've got a tough road ahead of you. If you couldn't live by your father's rules before, what makes you think you can live by them now? Oh, you might live by them for a while simply out of joy of being able to eat, take a bath, and have a roof over your head. But mark my words, before too long you'll be just as miserable as you were the first time from all the rules, all the work, and all the confinements that will keep you from what you really want to be doing in life. Moreover, you'll have to live with the leverage your father's going to have over you knowing you don't have any inheritance. Anytime you make a mistake, he'll bring it all up again of how you'll be back on the streets in no time if you don't obey."

"Why not just seek out a new life separate from your father? Get a job and live the life you want to live because it's going to be too hard for you to live under your father's rules."

With that, Discouragement continued his journey. The last thing he said from a distance was, "It's going to be too hard to live that way."

WILL IT BE TOO HARD?

Prod begin to think about all the rules he had previously rebelled against and thought to himself, *"Is it going to be too hard to live under my father's rules again? Am I going to be miserable once I've been there awhile? Why did I find it hard to obey his rules to begin with? Perhaps that guy was right; it is going to be too hard. Maybe I should just seek a life separate from my father. I don't have to go back to live in that riotous lifestyle. I can settle down here and start a new life."*

As he was pondering this, sitting under the shade tree, another fellow traveler was passing by. This traveler would tip the scales for Prod one way or the other.

IT'S NOT TOO HARD

If you think living for God is too hard, you're wrong. If you truly love God from your heart, His commands are not burdensome. It's when you're heart is not truly devoted to Him that His commands become heavy. It is then that you're trying to obey God out of obligation and not dedication. When you obey God out of obligation, it will make you miserable.

Loving God means keeping his commandments,
and his commandments are not burdensome.

1 John 5:3 (NLT)

"If you love Me, keep My commandments.

John 14:15 (NKJV)

Come to Me, all *you* who labor and are heavy
laden, and I will give you rest. Take My yoke
upon you and learn from Me, for I am gentle
and lowly in heart, and you will find rest for
your souls. For My yoke *is* easy and my burden
is light."

Matt 11:28–30 (NKJV)

THERE'S A REASON WHY IT'S HARD TO OBEY GOD

If you find obeying God becoming harder and harder, it's
because your relationship with God is getting colder and
colder. Keep your relationship with God fresh everyday and
you'll find that obedience to Him is not that hard. For the
prodigal, he must make up his mind that he's going to love
God with all he's got and not for all he can get.

The Journey Home–Part 5

Luke 15:11–24

The Traveler That Tipped the Scales

As Prod sat there, thinking about what the previous traveler, Discouragement, had said another traveler was passing by.

The traveler wasn't going to stop, but as he did a double take at Prod, he stopped.

"Prod, is that you?" the man said. Prod looked up and realized it was a friend of his father's. The man came over to where Prod was. "It is you!" the friend exclaimed.

Prod hung his head in shame.

"Prod, what has happened to you? Do you know your father has been worried sick about you ever since the day you left home"?

With that, Prod lifted his head in surprise and hope.

The Hope

"Everyday your father walks out to the edge of farm to see if he can see you coming down the road, and everyday he walks back to the house with heaviness upon his heart. He wonders everyday if you know how much he dearly loves you."

With that, tears began to flow down Prod's face.

"But how can my father still love me when I've been so rebellious and brought so much shame upon myself and him? I know I have no right to be accepted back into the family. How can he love me when I said such horrible things to him the day I stormed out of his life?"

"That's the miracle of love," said this family friend. "Love doesn't give us what we really deserve in times like this, rather what we don't deserve, forgiveness."

THE CHOICE

"Prod, you can live your life outside the father's house and you can die outside the father's house. You can live your life the way you want, separate from your father, but you will die in utter misery because you know you've rejected your father's love. You'll never be able to find anything that will replace your father's love for you. You will die never again experiencing your father's love. But Prod, you don't have to. Your father is waiting for you to journey back home to him. Come on, I'm going in that direction and I'll help you back home to your father."

HELPING HAND

With that, the friend of the family helped Prod to his feet. Every step they took closer to home Prod became more and more nervous. Prod's clothes were torn, stained and tattered. He hadn't had a bath in over a month, he stunk ,and he didn't even have any shoes. Prod was still going to confess to his father that he had sinned against heaven and him and was not worthy to be called his son anymore. Just simply make him a servant and that would be more than just for him to do.

When they got to the crossroads the friend of the family said, "Well Prod you know where this road leads, just a few miles in that direction and you'll be home. I'm sure you're father will be looking for you. He's going to be overjoyed to see you. Remember, he loves you dearly."

With that, the friend headed in the other direction and left Prod to make the final steps home.

ARE YOU A FRIEND OF A PRODIGAL?

When you find the prodigal, are you going to be as the friend in this story? Are you going to help him find his way home or are you going to just pass on by on the road of life? You could be the friend that tips the scales that bring the prodigal home. The end of the story would probably be different if that friend hadn't stopped that day to help this wayward child back home.

> Brethren, if anyone among you wanders from the truth, and someone turns him back, [20]let him know that he who turns a sinner from the error of his way will save a soul from death and cover a multitude of sins.
>
> James 5:19–20 (NKJV)

> The fruit of the righteous is a tree of life, and he who wins souls is wise.
>
> Prov 11:30 (NKJV)

> Brethren, if a man is overtaken in any trespass, you who are spiritual restore such a one in a spirit of gentleness, considering yourself lest you also be tempted.
>
> Gal 6:1 (NKJV)

You could be the one that tips the scales for eternity in a prodigal's life. Never give up because the prodigal may be at the point of simply needing a friend to help him make the final steps on his journey home.

THE JOURNEY HOME–PART 6
LUKE 15:11–24

THE FINAL STEPS OF HIS JOURNEY

Nervous and with tears streaming down his face, the prodigal slowly made his way towards the father's farm. With such internal conflict, he struggled with each step. The words of Livea, Liar, Condemnation, and Discouragement echoed through his mind. Each step was made in conflict with wanting to turn back and not face his father. A couple of times he turned to go back but saw the friend of the family still standing at the crossroads shaking his head "no" and pointing towards his father's farm. So he pressed on.

COULD IT BE?

While Prod was some distance away, the father, overseeing the workers in the fields, saw this pathetic figure of a man walking down the road. The father squinted his eyes in the noonday sun. The stature and swagger of this man looked familiar to the father. The father began to walk towards the road still squinting his eyes. The man on the road had his head down. However, when Prod lifted up his head, the father's eyes shot open with a look of absolute surprise coming upon his face.

A FATHER'S SHAME

"My son! My son! It's my son! He's come home!" With that, every worker in the field stopped what they were doing and looked in that direction. They saw the father lifting up his garment to his thighs, which was a sight of great shame in their custom, and running as hard as he could towards this prodigal child. A couple of the father's servants ran behind him. As the father reached his son, he grabbed him in a big bear hug and began kissing him on the cheek. It didn't matter to the father that his son stunk and was covered in mud or that his clothes were soiled from the refuse of the pigpen. All that mattered to him was his son, who was considered dead, was alive and back home.

A SON'S REPENTANCE

Once the father had loosened his grip a bit, the prodigal fell to his knees before the father and stated "father I have sinned greatly against heaven and against you, and I am no longer worthy to be called your son ... " In mid sentence, the father picked up his son and said to the servants standing there, "Bring my son some shoes, bring him the family robe and put the family ring upon his finger. Kill the fatted calf and let's celebrate, for my son that was dead is alive again."

GOD'S SHAME

Jesus hung in great shame on the cross for you and I. He hung there naked and bleeding for our sins. The Father has great love for you and I. If you are a prodigal, know that the Father has willingly shamed himself to run to you. The question is: Are you going to run to Him or run from Him.

The Father loves you dearly and wants you to feel His loving embrace. If you will run to Him in repentance and godly sorrow, you will find the Father's forgiveness and acceptance.

THE FATHER'S RESTORATION

Notice in this story of the prodigal that the father restored the son to full sonship. He gave him shoes to walk in life a lot easier, a robe identifying him as a rightful family member, and a ring of authority to conduct business on the father's behalf.

Though the journey back home for the prodigal was not as easy as he thought it would be; he did make it. Any prodigal can, once they realize they are in sin and are willing to come back home to the Father.

> "But the father said to his servants, 'Bring out the best robe and put it on him, and put a ring on his hand and sandals on his feet. ²³And bring the fatted calf here and kill it, and let us eat and be merry; ²⁴for this my son was dead and is alive again; he was lost and is found.' And they began to be merry."
>
> Luke 15:22–24 (NKJV)

THE ADVOCATE–PART 1

2 COR 5:10; REV 20:11–15; ROM 14:11–12

And as it is appointed for men to die once, but after this the judgment,

Heb 9:27 (NKJV)

A DAY WE MUST ALL FACE

The Day of Judgment had arrived. Before the Throne of God were two tables, one the defense and the other the prosecution. The courtroom of heaven was jammed with angels and other's who had already had their day in court and some awaiting their day. James had been summoned to the court to stand trial before God.

As James was seated at the defense table, he looked over at the prosecution table and saw a lone figure wearing a hooded shroud so you couldn't see his face. Gabriel called the court to order.

"All rise. Judgment Day has come for James to appear

before God Almighty to give an account for his life lived on earth. God's judgments are true and final and there is no court of appeals. What He speaks is the final word on this matter. He will hear both sides of this case and then make His final judgment." God entered the courtroom and sat upon His great throne.

THE PROSECUTION'S CASE

When the gavel hit to start the trial, the lone figure sitting at the prosecution's table immediately shot up. "Your Honor this man is guilty of not just one offense but multiple offenses."

With that, the prosecutor removed his hood, it was Satan himself. The devil began to tediously expound upon every sin that James had ever committed. As the long list of sins was expounded upon before God, James hung his head in shame. Tears began to flow down his face and onto the defense table. On and on the devil ranted and raved about the sinfulness of James' life he lived on earth.

With the prosecution wrapping up its case against James, the devil pointed an accusing finger at James and said, "Your honor this vile sinner cannot deny not one of these charges for he knows them to be true. Therefore, he stands guilty as charged and deserves nothing but the worst punishment for such heinous sins against you. He deserves eternal death!"

THE EVIDENCE IS TRUE!

With that, there broke out a wave of whispers throughout the courtroom of heaven. Gabriel then spoke to the defense, "You may now make your case to defend yourself." James, still sitting at the table by himself, sat in stunned silence. His head hung down with eyes shifting back and forth scrambling in his thoughts to come up with something to say. He knew that every charge the devil had brought against him before God was true. He knew that he was guilty as charged.

"Well" said Gabriel, "how do you plead against the charges made against you before God Almighty?" James sat in utter silence shaking his head in dismay for he could not defend himself against the charges brought against him before God. In broken voice, he began to utter words that would condemn him for all eternity, "I'm … I'm … I'm … "

WHAT ABOUT YOU?

What would you be able to say in the face of all the charges of your sins? What is James going to do? He is facing eternal death with no court of appeals, this is the final judgment!

Why not stop a moment and reflect upon everything you're doing in the light of your appointment with the court of heaven called "judgment day."

> And as it is appointed for men to die once, but after this the judgment …
>
> Heb 9:27 (NKJV)

THE ADVOCATE–PART 2

2 COR 5:10; REV 20:11–15; ROM 14:11–12

And as it is appointed for men to die once, but after this the judgment...

Heb 9:27 (NKJV)

"Well," said Gabriel, "how do you plead against the charges made against you before God Almighty?" James sat in utter silence shaking his head in dismay for he could not defend himself against the charges brought against him before God. In broken voice, he began to utter words that would condemn him for all eternity, "I'm... I'm... I'm..."

THE ADVOCATE

"Not guilty!" said a voice from off to the side. "He's not guilty your Honor." The courtroom was immediately filled with low whispers of disbelief. James looked up to see who had declared such a statement when all the evidence proved otherwise. From the crowd stepped forward Jesus the advocate of God's children.

"Your Honor it is true that James committed all those sins that were brought to the attention of this Court. However, what the prosecution failed to mention was the fact that James came to me with a repentant heart and asked me to forgive him of his sins. That day he made a commitment from his heart to follow Me and allow Me to be the LORD of His life. While not perfect, as none will be, each time the Holy Spirit dealt with him about sin and shortcomings in his life, he asked for forgiveness and strength to live a life pleasing to Me. Therefore your Honor, I offer My blood as payment for the penalty of his crimes against You and because of that he be declared not guilty for all eternity."

"*Not fair!*" screamed the devil. "With the advocate's own words He declared before this court that James had committed all the crimes brought to light this day. This court cannot find anything but guilt for this man, he's guilty as charged! In fact, look in the book of records for the life of James and you will see clearly recorded all his sins."

THE BOOKS ARE OPENED

With that, the books were opened, the Word of God, the record of James' life and the Lamb's Book of Life. God reviewed the record of James life from cover to cover and then closed the book and handed it to Gabriel. "The sins that the prosecution brought against James to this court are not found in the record of his life, not one of them."

"What!" exclaimed the devil. "I have a copy all the records of his life right here! I have the dates, the times, the locations, and the exact nature of each and every sin. I have it all right here! Let me see that book," the devil demanded. As he looked through heaven's record of James life, the devil became confused and then frantic. He compared heaven's record with his own. Every place in heaven's record that there was supposed to be a sin recorded was covered with a red substance yet transparent, and nothing could be seen beneath it.

"What is this?" snarled the devil.

"It's none other than the blood of My Son the advocate, to all who call upon Him for forgiveness of their sins," replied God. With that, the devil dropped the book and stepped back in repulse and fear.

"Your Honor," spoke the advocate, "look in My book, the Lamb's Book of Life and You will see James' name inscribed therein."

With that, Gabriel looked through the pages of The Lamb's Book of Life. As he was scanning the pages with his finger, he stopped and a smile sprung upon his face. "Indeed Your Honor, James' name is inscribed in The Lamb's Book of Life."

THE FINAL JUDGMENT RENDERED

The gavel of God swung and landed with a thunderous and final declaration, "Not guilty by the blood of the Lamb!"

With that, the courtroom of heaven erupted in celebration and the devil, furious, stormed out of the courtroom. James collapsed into the arms of Jesus with sobs of joys and gratefulness. Jesus whispered into the ear of James, "Well done my good and faithful servant, enter into the joys of the LORD."

WILL YOU HAVE THE ADVOCATE AT YOUR TABLE?

We are all sinners, not one of us can defend ourselves against the charges brought against us before God, but thanks be to God for the precious blood of Jesus! His blood will wash away *all* our sins! Nevertheless, for that blood to be applied to your life, you have to ask Jesus to forgive you of your sins. Make a heart-felt commitment to *stop* the sins you are asking for forgiveness for. You must commit to obey Jesus by obeying the Word of God. Once you do that and you sin thereafter, when the Holy Spirit brings that sin to your attention, again ask Jesus to forgive and wash you from that sin.

> If we say that we have no sin, we deceive ourselves, and the truth is not in us. [9]If we confess our sins, He is faithful and just to forgive us our sins and to cleanse us from all unrighteousness.
>
> 1 John 1:8–9 (NKJV)

THE ADVOCATE–PART 3

EPH 2:8–9; ISA 64:6; PHIL 2:21; JOHN 3:3–21

The day of judgment had arrived. Before the throne of God were two tables, one the defense and the other the prosecution. The courtroom of heaven was jammed with angels and other's who had already had their day in court. Tom had been summoned to the court to stand trial before God.

As Tom was seated at the defense table, he looked over at the prosecution table and saw a lone figure wearing a hooded shroud so you couldn't see his face. Gabriel called the court to order.

"All rise. Judgment Day has come for Tom to appear before God Almighty to give an account for his life lived on earth. God's judgments are true and final and there is no court of appeals. What He speaks is the final word on this matter. He will hear both sides of this case and then make His final judgment." God entered the courtroom and sat upon His great throne.

Tom had witnessed the previous trial of James so when the gavel hit Tom immediately shot up to declare his case before the prosecution had a chance.

DEFENSE GIVES ITS CASE FIRST

"Your Honor I will gladly stand and give an account of my life lived on earth. While I, as all others, was not perfect, as was stated by the advocate in the previous case, I was a good man." With that, Tom began to state his case before God.

"I was Boy Scout and achieved the highest ranking. Throughout my schooling, I was always on the honor roll. I was given numerous awards throughout my school years for citizenship, help, good deeds, and good sportsmanship. I was voted most likely to succeed, of which you will see in my case that I did indeed live up to those expectations.

"I received a graduate degree and was the valedictorian in my high school, under graduate and graduate schools. I was on the dean's list every semester throughout my illustrious collegiate career. I worked two and three jobs to pay my way through college. I worked as a volunteer in nursing homes, toy drives for underprivileged children, three different civic organizations and I even went to church once and a while.

"I excelled in my career field and was given numerous awards of achievement and excellence. I was a faithful husband and father, making sure that I worked long and hard to supply for them. I was financially frugal and upon my death had several million dollars accrued of which 2% went to charitable organization upon my death. I was a model citizen for all to see."

DEFENSE RESTS ITS CASE

"Your Honor, if more people were like me, the world would definitely be a better place to live. I tried to set the example but it's up to them to follow it. I just don't see how the prosecution will be able to defame me before this court. The record of my life will show all these things I have spoken in my defense to be true. With that Your Honor I rest my case."

With that, all eyes of heaven's courtroom turned to the lone figure seated at the prosecution table. The shrouded figure stood to his feet.

THE ADVOCATE–PART 4

EPH 2:8–9; ISA 64:6; PHIL 2:21; JOHN 3:3–21

Tom has just given, before the court of heaven, a resounding defense of his life. A defense of which deserves the reward of heaven. He has plenty of evidence to support his defense and was very confident that the court would find him "not-guilty" of any crime the prosecution was about to accuse him of. Tom was in the courtroom audience when the prosecutor, the devil, vehemently accused James of the most heinous crimes against God. However, Tom was sure that by jumping up first to present his case, essentially the prosecutor would not have a case.

A BIZARRE TWIST

As Tom was seated with a confident smirk across his face, the prosecutor stood. "Your Honor this man is guilty of the blood of Your Son." With that, the prosecutor removed the hood from his head and Tom gasped in unbelief, it was Jesus.

"While it is true that Tom did all those good deeds he did not once do it for the glory of God. When the Holy Spirit confronted him about his sins and the need to repent and ask Me for forgiveness he would not relent. He pardoned himself by doing more good deeds. Time after time, the Holy Spirit would plead with him to admit his sins and repent of them, but he would have none of that. He scoffed at the idea that he truly needed to repent, because of all the good deeds he was doing. He rejected My sacrifice for his sins and therefore rejected all hope for forgiveness. You, o God, have said that man's attempt to be declared good before You is like filth soiled putrefying rags that make you sick.

"Remember, o God, that day that I came before You with My blood and sprinkled it upon Your throne. I went to earth and lived a life without sin so humanity could have one that could be *the* representative for all humanity. I fulfilled the righteous requirements that You required of all men but none could attain because of sin. You accepted My life and My blood as complete and final payment for all sins.

THE STANDARD

Your Honor, the standard has been set that one must be born again for entrance into heaven. To be born again is to have one's sins forgiven. For this forgiveness to be applied to one's life they must admit to You that they are a sinner and unable to save themselves; nor are they able to be good enough on their own to be acceptable to You. They must ask me to forgive them of all their sins. They must surrender their life to Me and commit with their heart to follow Me the rest of the days of their life. Tom never did this. Look in the book of his life, for you will not find My blood applied to his life."

SURELY NOT!

"But Your Honor," interrupted Tom, "I have lived a good life. I never murdered anyone, I was faithful to my marriage, well more faithful than most. I was a good father, why my boys made varsity because I spent many a Sunday practicing with them. Surely you see all the good I have done far outweighs any sin I have done. I mean even Jesus admitted when James stood before you that none will ever be perfect."

With that, God looked through the book of Tom's life from cover to cover. "I see your sins glaring out to me and your good deeds smell as filth."

IS YOUR NAME IN THAT BOOK?

"Your Honor, look in My book of life and you will not find his name written therein. Gabriel, look in the Lamb's Book of Life to see if Tom's name is written therein."

Gabriel scanned with his finger through the book cover to cover shaking his head no. "But wait a minute! I know my name has to be in that book. I've been too good of a person. When you compare my life and James' life, I lived a much better life than he and his name was in that Book."

Gabriel scanned again cover to cover and shook his head no.

JUDGMENT HAS BEEN RENDERED

With that, the gavel of God's judgment fell with a thunderous judgment of "Guilty as charged! Depart from me you worker of iniquity! You are hereby sentenced to eternal death." The courtroom of heaven was immediately filled with gasps and whispers of those in attendance. Two angles came and began to escort Tom from the courtroom to meet his fate.

As Tom was being escorted out he was screaming, "No! No! It can't be! I was told that all I had to do was be good and I'd go to heaven! I was told that all I had to do was believe that there was a God and I'd go to heaven! No! I deserve to go to heaven! I worked hard at being and doing good! No! No!" Tom's voice faded as he was taken from the courtroom to meet his eternal fate.

Is He Your Advocate or Your Prosecutor?

The twist in this story is that for those who are not born again the prosecutor is Jesus because He is the Word and the Word will condemn those who are not born again. Say and think what you want, but the fact remains that the Word will either be your advocate or your judge. He is an advocate to those who in this life have called upon Him for forgiveness and live in conscious obedience to Him, but for those who do not do as such; He will be the prosecutor and judge.

> For as the Father has life in himself, so He has granted the Son to have life in himself, ²⁷and has given Him authority to execute judgment also, because He is the Son of Man.
>
> John 5:26–27 (NKJV)

> ¹My dear children, I am writing this to you so that you will not sin. But if anyone does sin, we have an Advocate who pleads our case before the Father. He is Jesus Christ, the one who is truly righteous. ²He Himself is the sacrifice that atones for our sins—and not only our sins but the sins of all the world. ³And we can be sure that we know Him if we obey his commandments. ⁴If someone claims, "I know God," but doesn't obey God's commandments, that person is a liar and is not living in the truth.
>
> 1 John 2:1–4 (NLT)

LIFE

JAMES 4:14; PSA 90:12

IT'S MONDAY MORNING

It's Monday morning and he had hurried out the door as he did most mornings, but so did his wife and kids on their way to work and school. His thoughts were consumed with his presentation he was to give that midmorning. It had been a beautiful spring weekend. His wife and kids had wanted to take a picnic to the park, but he couldn't because the presentation was too important and he had to put all he could into preparing for it. He even sent his wife and kids to church and stayed home to work on it. Why if he did a good job on this presentation it was assured that it would secure his promotion in the company.

A PLAUSIBLE SITUATION

He was taking his normal route to work and as he hurriedly approached one of the intersections, something out of the corner of this left eye caught his attention. It was a cement truck running the red light at the intersection. At that milli-second, everything was in super slow motion. He knew that he was about to be in a sure death auto accident and there was nothing he could do about it.

At that millisecond what was going through his mind, his presentation he had worked so hard on? Was he think-ing, "*How is the company ever going survive without me?*" Was he thinking about that promotion he would have received if he had given that presentation?

What would you be thinking about at that millisecond? Would you be thinking about all your education and degrees you've earned? Would you be thinking about your retire-ment plan? Would you be thinking about the accolades that you had received at your job? I doubt it but if so, you've completely missed out on what life is all about!

Now this is a hypothetical situation but a very plausi-ble one. Over the next few chapters, I want you to join me to stop and look at what's important in life and to look at whether or not we have our priorities right.

LIFE... WHAT'S IT ALL ABOUT?

The millisecond is over and the horrific sound of the cement truck crashing into the driver's side reverberates in his ear... Life—what's it really all about?

> [14]*whereas you do not know what will happen tomorrow. For what is your life? It is even a vapor that appears for a little time and then vanishes away.*
>
> *James 4:14 (NKJV)*

> [12] *So teach us to number our days, that we may gain a heart of wisdom.*
>
> *Psa 90:12 (NKJV)*

LIFE...HOW MANY DAYS?

Based upon last chapter's devotional "Life" and it bringing into sharp focus how quickly life can come to an end I give the following:

One of my associates walked into my office at about 11:30 a.m. and told me to turn on the TV to the news channel. What I saw caused perplexity to fill my mind. Over thirty innocent college students met their tragic fate from the idiotic whim of a crazed gunman. I don't know how much clearer my devotional from yesterday could have rang any truer in my mind.

THE REALITY OF IT

Not to place any phobic fear in anyone, but unexpected death can and does come to millions every day. Those college students, most of who were probably in their 20's, were not thinking about the end of their life that day. What was the last twenty-four hours of their life like? What was the last conversation they had with their friends and loved ones? Did they have what now would definitely be a frivolous argument with a parent, a friend, a fiancé or fiancée, spouse ... ?

A Life Ahead of Them

They were planning their life and planning for success in their future careers. They were preparing to live a long life. They were planning on careers that would bring them satisfactory income. They were planning to live the "American Dream" perhaps.

Focus

Our lives are consumed by so many things that lead us to be distracted from what's really important in life. I know my life has been and is too distracted from what's really important. I personally know of preachers that have dropped dead or have met an untimely and tragic death in the "prime" of their life.

Stop!

Stop a moment and meditate upon these Scriptures. No, stop, clear your mind, take 5 undistracted minutes, and ponder what these Scriptures are saying.

> Come now, you who say, "Today or tomorrow we will go to such and such a city, spend a year there, buy and sell, and make a profit"; [14]whereas you do not know what will happen tomorrow. For what is your life? It is even a vapor that appears for a little time and then vanishes away. [15]Instead you ought to say, "If the LORD wills, we shall live and do this or that." [16]But now you boast in your arrogance. All such boasting is evil.
>
> James 4:13–16 (NKJV)

So teach us to number our days, That we may
gain a heart of wisdom.

Psa 90:12 (NKJV)

Our hearts and prayers go out to the VA Tech families who
lost loved ones in this tragic shooting on VA Tech campus.

CAREFUL HOW YOU FILL IN THE BLANKS

EPH 4:1–6; JAMES 3:4–18; 1 COR 1:10–11

> For where envy and self-seeking exist, confusion
> and every evil thing are there.
>
> James 3:16 (NKJV)

Sunday morning the church was a buzz with confusion. You could feel the tension in the air. It was a tight and anxious feeling. You could scan through the crowd and see some talking in whispered tones with angry scowls upon their face. Some were in whispered tones with "can you believe it, why I've never..." Some were looks of absolute confusion looking to and fro trying to make sense of the whole situation.

The crowd came to a slow hush as the pastor stepped into the pulpit. With tears streaming down his face and his voice broken with emotion he spoke with meekness.

AN AWFUL THING

"Something awful has happened to this congregation this week. Someone allowed the devil to fill in the blanks in their minds over a situation. Through their misinterpretation they began to report something as truth that was a lie. It has been reported that I am having an affair."

THE BLANK FILLED IN

"This report comes from someone who, passing by my office one day this past week, looked through the window in my door and saw me hugging a beautiful young woman. From that the blank that was filled in was, 'the pastor must be having an affair.'"

"I heed the Biblical warning of 'abstaining from the very appearance of evil.' Therefore, I do not hug women I am not related to. This young lady came to my office in tears and broken over the news she had just received from the doctors of her two year old son. That news was that her two year old boy was diagnosed with an advanced stage of Leukemia. She knew that she was away from God and was ready to come back to Him.

THE MYSTERY WOMAN

This young lady that I was saw hugging in my office is my sister's daughter, my niece. She's more like a daughter to me than a niece. I watched her grow up and as a child through early teens she was literally on fire for God. I also watched in heartache as she walked away from God as a teenager because of unfounded rumors and judgments about her youth pastor, which caused dissention in the youth group. I have wept with my sister on more than one occasion for God to reach her and bring her back to Him. This week God was bringing her back to Him. I willingly embraced my loved one because she was hurt, afraid, and repentant.

When the news of this awful and unfounded rumor

was reported to me, my immediate thoughts were not of my reputation but of my niece. With all the hurt from her youth over "church people" using their tongues to spread judgments and dissention, would she stay with God or once again walk away dismayed over "Christians"?

WHAT'S THE FOCUS?

It appears that those who allow their tongues to be used to spread rumors, dissention, and judgment are not at all concerned about Christ's command and commission to the church and His followers. "Look unto the harvest fields and bring in the harvest." These individuals are inward focused trying to find the faults of others rather than seeking to save the lost. Folks, no one has to look very long to find plenty of faults. We will all have them and will continue to until we reach heaven.

PROMOTING THE DEVILS SCHEME

Do you see how easy it is for us to fall prey to the devil's tactics to fill in the blanks? But what's worse than allowing the devil to fill in the blanks, is to use our tongue to promote such. At the very least, instead of going to others that person should have come to me and questioned me about what they saw. I could have accurately filled in the blanks and none of this horrible event would have happened.

CASTING THE FIRST STONE

However, I do not stand here today to cast a condemning stone at you. I, like the Pharisees when questioned by Jesus, "he who is without sin let him cast the first stone," cannot cast one. I too have at times allowed the devil to fill in the blanks and I didn't pursue the truth to verify the answer I filled in the blank with.

THE LESSON TO LEARN

May we all learn not to fill in the blanks without testing the validity and truthfulness of the answers to which we ascribe to those blanks. May we learn to hold our tongue in subjection to Christ and keep our eyes outward to the harvest."

> "He who loves purity of heart ... has grace on his lips,"
>
> Prov 22:11a (NKJV).

I Can Handle It

Judges 16:1–21; James 1:12–15

Wagon Driver Needed

The story goes that back in the 1800's a mining company needed to hire a driver to drive a wagonload of nitroglycerin through a very narrow and winding mountain road. The previous several drivers had died when their wagons went over the side of the mountain. The pay was good but the danger was high. Three men showed up for the job interview. The supervisor took them one by one into a room for a private interview. He only asked one question, "How close to the edge can you put the wagon without it going over the side?"

The first man said, "I can put that wagon within two feet of the edge without it going over." The supervisor excused the man, called the next man in, and asked the same and only question. This man, with a tone of arrogance, said, "I'm so good I can put one wheel over the edge without going over." The supervisor excused the man and called in the final candidate. He asked him the same and only question. This man responded, "Because of the cargo I'm carrying and potential death I will keep the wagon as far away from the edge as possible." He was the one that got the job.

WHICH DRIVER ARE YOU?

When it comes to temptations which driver are you? You know the Adamic nature is easily fooled into believing that it can handle the temptation. Thus, it keeps flirting with it and getting closer and closer to the edge of disaster.

In Judges 16, we see Samson who seemed invincible. Apparently he thought so himself and kept flirting with disaster. You can see his arrogance from the fact that after the first time Delilah tried to trick him into revealing the secret of his strength, he stayed. Then after the second time, he stayed. Then she wove his hair into a weaver's beam, which is getting awful close to the truth of his strength, yet he stayed. You know the rest of the story.

HOW STUPID!

We look at Samson and say, "how arrogant, how stupid, how audacious ..." but yet how many of us have done or are doing the same thing? The Philistines physically blinded Samson by poking his eyes out, but Samson had become blind long before that. So we too can become blind to temptation, yet it is a blindness that we allow. In regards to temptation, we should all be as the third driver in our story. He respected the danger of the situation and stayed as far away as he could from that which would bring certain death.

> Temptation comes from our own desires, which entice us and drag us away. ¹⁵These desires give birth to sinful actions. And when sin is allowed to grow, it gives birth to death.
>
> *James* 1:14–15 *(NLT)*

If you are in the "weaver's beam" so to speak, ask Jesus to break you free and then flee that temptation. You cannot play with fire and not get burned, yet those who think they can are the very ones that get burned worst in the end.

HE KNEW NOT

JUDGES 16:19–20

Sleeping like a baby in the lap of the woman he loved, he was awakened by her words, "Samson! Samson! The Philistines are upon you!" So once again, he awoke and arose to go take care of business as he had done so many times. He had never been defeated by these uncircumcised Philistines and knew that he would make easy work of them.

A VERY SAD VERSE OF SCRIPTURE

Judges 16:20 is a very sad verse in the Bible. " ... But he did not know that the LORD had departed from him."

How did he come to the place where he didn't even know God's presence and power were no longer in his life? Better yet, what deceptive substitute caused him to think that the presence of God was still upon his life? As mentioned in our previous devotional Samson was flirting with temptation and continued to do so because he thought he could handle it. However, here's a probing question: How could he go from knowing the power and presence of God to not knowing His presence had left, yet believing it was still there?

IT STILL HAPPENS TODAY

Sadly, I have seen this same scenario happen to too many Christians and yes, even ministers. They once walked in the power and joy of Christ. They once basked in the presence of God. They once sought His presence. Their worship was a lifestyle and was a thing of beauty giving glory to God. They sought after God around the altars and experienced God's presence and grace and it was evident to all around. They once knew all this, but somehow substituted something in its place and began believing that the substitute was the real deal. How does a Christian get to this place?

LITTLE COMPROMISES

Just like Samson, they begin to justify little compromises of violating God's Word. Actually, Delilah was a *big* compromise because she was a Gentile that served foreign gods. They start missing church worship services to pursue other personal interest. That's just a little thing so they justify it. Then they start missing just a little bit more and justify it. Then they start entertaining themselves with stuff that appeals to the Adamic nature.

All along the way they are confronted by the Holy Spirit about their compromises. They resist and refuse to heed the Holy Spirit's convictions. Each time they do this they are hardening their spirit's sensitivity to the Holy Spirit, the presence of God.

SOOTHING THE CONSCIENCE

The question that still begs to be answered is: How can they not know that they are leaving God's presence? Each time they seek to justify their compromise, they are seeking for something to soothe their conscience. The devil offers soothing deception that when accepted is done so at the price of walking a bit further from the presence of God. Deception is when you act upon a lie that you think is the truth.

THE PRICE OF LEAVING GOD'S PRESENCE

Samson didn't realize it at first, but it became painfully clear that he had indeed walked from the presence of God when he was captured and placed in bondage. I too have seen many come to the shocking reality that they had indeed left the presence of God when sin's destructive seeds begin to produce the fruit of bondage and pain. Only then do they realize that they had bought into the devil's deception. That deception gives you a false security that you're still in God's presence.

HUMBLE OBSERVATION

Throughout my years of observation, I want to leave you with the following probing questions that may expose the fact that you too are leaving the presence of God.

How hungry are you for the presence of God? What are you willing to do or give up to seek His presence?

Are you justifying missing church? Are you justifying missing even more church?

Are you justifying not spending time reading the Word and being in prayer?

When are at a church worship service are you there just marking time or are you there to worship God from your heart and hear His Word?

Are you justifying your entertainment choices that really mock the standards of God's Word?

Are you justifying your desire to fellowship with sinners? (Note fellowshipping with and being a friend to sinners are two different things.)

Are you mad that I've even asked these questions?

[21] *Then the Philistines took him and put out his eyes, and*

brought him down to Gaza. They bound him with bronze fet-
ters, and he became a grinder in the prison.

Please, you don't have to go through the pain and bondage that deception and sin will bring. Don't even allow
yourself to compromise the values of God's Word. Don't
come to the place where you don't know that God's presence
as left you.

"*... But he did not know that the* LORD *had departed from*
him."

FROM SIN TO GRACE

JUDGES 16:22–30; 2 SAM 12:7–14; GAL 6:7–9

Day after day he trudged around attached to the grinding wheel of the Philistines. Every day people would come by to mock and spit upon him. Samson lived in darkness because his enemies had gouged out his eyes. This once mighty man of God, now reduced to a scorned slave, all of which the consequence of his sins. God said that He would not be mocked. If you sow to the flesh sin, you will reap the bitter harvest those seeds produce in your life.

IS THERE ANY HOPE?

Lest we leave Samson in the captivity and bondage without any hope, let's continue the story. Samson has faced the horrid reality that he had bought into the deceptions of temptation and sin that caused him to be in bondage. His enemies physically put his eyes out and chained him to the grinding wheel to grind the meal like an animal. Day after day he was forced to trudge in a monotonous circle, all while hearing those passing by yell at him and mock him. How many times did Samson replay the regrettable events in his mind that lead him to this state?

> "However, the hair of his head began to grow again after it had been shaven."
>
> Jdg. 16:22 (NKJV)

> "...But where sin abounded, grace abounded much more,"
>
> Rom 5:20 (NKJV)

FROM SIN TO GRACE

Yes, for those who have fallen prey to temptation and sin there is hope of finding God's grace once again. For those that truly repent with godly sorrow will find God's forgiveness and grace. Once they are forgiven, they are forgiven! They are the prodigal come home to a father that loves them and restores them to full son ship.

PRESUMPTUOUS

I must give a word of caution to those who may be facing or will face temptations to buy into sin. Please don't buy into this thought process, "I can partake of this sin and then ask God to forgive me." First of all, that's very presumptuous, because God will not be mocked; and secondly, there's always a physical, emotional, and sometimes social price to pay for buying into sin. Sometimes that price may linger for many years after you've found grace and forgiveness.

KING DAVID FOR EXAMPLE

Even though King David found grace and forgiveness with God, there was a long-term price, his family had to pay for his sins of adultery and murder. God said that the sword would never depart from David's house because of his sin. Here are some of the results: The newborn died, one of David's sons raped his half sister, one of David's sons murdered his half brother, and one of David's sons rose in rebellion and temporarily took over David's kingdom while David ran for his life. That same son was killed in battle.

Samson found grace, but because of his sins, it ultimately leads to his death.

WHY REPENT?

Okay, so why repent of sins if there's still an ill harvest to reap?

Do not be deceived, God is not mocked; for whatever a man sows, that he will also reap. ⁸For he who sows to his flesh will of the flesh reap corruption, *but he who sows to the Spirit will of the Spirit reap everlasting life.* ⁹And let us not grow weary while doing good, for in due season we shall reap if we do not lose heart. Gal 6:7–9 (NKJV)

Once you've repented, asked for, and received forgiveness, you can then begin to sow seeds of the Spirit, which is obedience to God's Word. Those seeds will begin to reap everlasting life! However, you cannot do that if you keep trudging in sin and sowing those seeds that produce an ill harvest.

THE GREATEST REASON

But the greatest reason to repent of your sins and ask for forgiveness is you enter into a relationship with God and there's nothing sweeter than that. Though your flesh may reap what was sown in sin your spirit and soul will be free in Christ and it's a freedom you can feel! You keep sowing seeds of the Spirit and you will have a bountiful harvest of *life*!

ARE YOU STRUGGLING?

If you are struggling with reaping what was sown in sin, let me tell that God's grace is sufficient to carry you through this. Secondly, be sure that what you're struggling with is not condemnation. The devil cannot stand the fact that you've been forgiven and have the possibility of *life*. Therefore, he is going to keep reminding you of your past sins and keep telling you that you cannot live a life pleasing to God. Remember, the devil is liar and that he lied to you in the first place to buy into sin. You keep walking in obedience to God's Word and any time you slip immediately, ask for forgiveness, pick yourself up, and keep walking with God.

"And let us not grow weary while doing good, for in due season we shall reap if we do not lose heart." Gal 6:9 (NKJV)

Genuine Faith Part 1

2 Tim 1:5–7; Gen 39–41

He was awakened by the crack of a whip and the simultaneous screams of painful agony. He closed his eyes in repulse, as his nose caught a whiff of the horrid stench of raw open sewage mixed with the pungent smell of sweaty un-bathed body order. A few nights before, he was sleeping in relative comfort being the house manager for one of the most powerful man in the country. This morning he is a common prisoner.

His thoughts turned to the dreams of God's promises he'd had so many years ago. Joseph did nothing worthy of being sold into slavery. He was in prison because he did what was right in God's eyes. He resisted the temptations of sexual immorality presented to him by Potiphar's wife. She falsely accused him of rape because he literally ran from her presence when she was determined to force him to give in.

Further From God's Promises

His current situation seemingly put him even further from the fulfillment of God's dreams and promises for his life.

I'm sure the devil was there screaming in his ear to blame God for all this. Joseph had a choice to make: Give up or hold on to his faith.

We see that Joseph chose to have faith in God rather than give into the despair that pressed upon his soul through the circumstances around him. But how could he have faith in God when everything in the natural screamed that God had forsaken him?

HOW CAN YOU HAVE THIS KIND OF FAITH?

When you've done everything right but it still falls apart; when you've lived right according to God's Word; when you've prayed and fasted and wept before God and it doesn't seem that anything is happening on your behalf; there's seemingly nothing moving you closer to the fulfillment of God's promises for your life; when it seems that your circumstances are thrusting you further into the darkness of despair; you have a choice: Give up or hold on to your faith.

YOU HAVE TO HAVE GENUINE FAITH.

> ⁵when I call to remembrance the genuine faith that is in you, which dwelt first in your grandmother Lois and your mother Eunice, and I am persuaded is in you also.

In our next chapter, I'll show you how to have this *genuine* faith that can withstand anything life can dish out. In the meantime, I would ask that you read Genesis chapters 39–41.

I will also tell you that the key to this type of faith is to understand what the Greek word for *genuine* means in 1 Tim 1:5.

Don't give up! You too can have this kind of faith! You too can make it through anything life can dish out.

Genuine Faith Part 2

2 Tim 1:5–7; Gen 39–41

Continued from Part 1

When you've done everything right but it still falls apart; when you've lived right according to God's Word; when you've prayed and fasted and wept before God and it doesn't seem that anything is happening on your behalf; there's seemingly nothing moving you closer to the fulfillment of God's promises for your life; when it seems that your circumstances are thrusting you further into the darkness of despair; you have a choice: Give up or hold on to your faith.

How can you have this kind of faith?

You have to have *genuine* faith.

⁵when I call to remembrance the genuine faith that is in you, which dwelt first in your grandmother Lois and your mother Eunice, and I am persuaded is in you also.

The Greek word for *genuine* means, "undisguised, non-hypocritical, non-dissembled, that is, sincere: without dissimulation." In other words, it's not mixed with pollutants. Faith is so powerful that it can withstand anything life can dish out, but it has to be *genuine* faith. You cannot mix faith with sin. You cannot mix faith with doubt. You cannot mix faith with compromise. You cannot mix faith with disobedience. You cannot mix faith with selfishness.

What Builds Genuine Faith?

Our growing relationship with God grows *genuine* faith. A growing relationship is defined as one that includes time in His Word, time in communing with Him in prayer and living out obedience to God. In that growing relationship, God will show you things that you are mixing with your faith that need to be removed from the mix. God will also pour His Word and His Spirit into your life to build your faith.

One Final Ingredient

There's one more ingredient that God pours into the mix of *genuine* faith, tests. Faith untested is weak faith. God will allow and/or take the circumstances of life and use them to test our faith. He will not allow us to be burdened with more than we can bear.

> No temptation has overtaken you except such as is common to man; but God is faithful, who will not allow you to be tempted beyond what you are able, but with the temptation will also make the way of escape, that you may be able to bear it.
>
> 1 Cor 10:13 (NKJV)

I've been there when the circumstances of life were so painful that all I could do in my prayer time was weep before God and say, "It hurts God; it hurts." I can look back and see that during that time of tremendous testing,

God was there carrying me through. I shudder to think what would have happened and where I'd be today if I had given up on my faith.

THE MAIN INGREDIENT THAT WE ADD IS…

The main ingredient that we have to add is action. We must act upon our faith for it to be genuine. Act meaning obey, do what the Word says to do. Live it out in practical everyday living.

What about you, is your faith *genuine*? Are you mixing your faith with pollutants? The only thing that builds *genuine* faith is the purity of God's Word and your faithful and loving obedience to do what His Word says to do.

"⁵when I call to remembrance the genuine faith that is in you …"

DOES JESUS HAVE YOUR LUNCH?

JOHN 6:4-13

Johnny hopped out of bed, put his exploring clothes on, and picked up his lunch basket that mom had made for him. His mom was used to him exploring the near by hillsides every-day so she made him a lunch everyday. Nothing exciting ever happened in his remote little village. There was noth-ing but miles of hillsides to explore. He would catch bugs, small reptiles, and other things that make boys, boys.

He was couple of miles outside the village exploring the hills and as he topped one of those hills, he saw something that made him do a double take. Out here in the middle of nowhere were thousands of people. He rubbed his eyes and squinted with his hand over his forehead to block the noon-day sun. They all seemed to be huddled around something.

As Johnny was making his way through the crowd, he heard a stern voice and a firm hand grab him by the arm. "Hey boy, what do you have in that basket of yours?" He looked up at the man that had him by the arm. The man's face was weathered and gruff looking, but not old. Johnny was speechless. "Well, what do you have in your basket?" The gruff man insisted. "It's my lunch...I'll share with you if you'd like," Johnny replied. "What is it?" the man questioned. "Let me see what my mama packed me today...I have two small fish and five rolls." Johnny was hoping that the meager meal would be a turn off for the gruff man, but the man, still holding Johnny by the arm said, "come with me."

The gruff man lead Johnny through the sea of people. They came to a clearing in the midst of this sea of people to find a lone man sitting on a large rock. "Master," said the gruff man, "we have looked throughout the entire crowd of people and all we have is this little boy's lunch of two fish and five rolls, but what is that compared too so many people," he questioned.

Johnny looked up at the man sitting on the large rock. Unlike the man holding him by the arm, this man had a smile on his face and a twinkle in his eye. "Come," said and motioned the friendly man on the large rock. With that, the gruff man released Johnny to bid the master's calling. The closer Johnny came the better he felt because this man had a presence of peace about him that was not felt within the crowd.

When he arrived where the man was, the man stretched out his arms, picked Johnny up, sat him in his lap, and gave him a big hug. "We need a miracle today, we have to feed all these people," said the man. Johnny looked around at the sea of hungry faces and looked back into the eyes of his new friend. "Where are you going to get all that food," inquired Johnny. "Why from you of course," the man said. Johnny's eyes got big and then He chuckled a bit and said, "Sir, I think you greatly underestimate my mother's cooking." The man chuckled too and said, "Well, if you will give me all your lunch I can make it feed all these people, and then some."

~

Do you ever use your imagination when reading the Bible? I am not talking about using it to interpret the Bible but to put yourself there in the scene. I try to do that when possible, because it adds another dimension to the Bible. As you read this story of the little boy with five loaves and two fish, put yourself in the story as the little boy. From this story, I want to relate some powerful truths that apply to us today, in that Jesus wants your lunch.

THE NEED IS BIGGER THAN YOUR PROVISIONS

There are several dynamic and powerful lessons that are taught in this one event. First, there was a need that was too big for the disciples to meet. They looked to Jesus to solve the problem, but Jesus put it back on their shoulders, so to speak. When they inventoried their resources, they realized that what they had fell grossly short of what was needed. Precisely! We will never have enough on our own to meet the needs around us.

JESUS NEEDS YOUR LUNCH

Another dynamic lesson is that Jesus needs what we've got to meet the needs of those around us. Sure, Jesus could have had the angles crank up the manna oven and rain down manna, but Jesus was teaching us something extremely important: faith and sacrifice. The boy had to give Jesus all his lunch or else this story would not have been as it is. Jesus didn't ask for part of the lunch, but all of it. Jesus wants all your lunch.

BLESSED AND BROKEN

Another dynamic this story teaches us is when you give your frail, inept abilities to Jesus, he will receive them, bless them, break them and give them back with miracle provision. Wow, there's a whole other devotional just on that one dynamic.

Imagine Being a Disciple

Now put yourself in the story as one of the disciples. You've just been handed a small piece of bread and a smaller piece of fish and you've been told to turn around and feed thousands. Are you looking into your hands and seeing the bread and the fish? Are you looking out at the thousands of hungry people waiting for *you* to feed them? Ok, you're walking to the first group of people and have this uncomfortable smile on your face as you reach down and break off half of your bread and fish and hand it to the first person. You squint your eyes and look down at the bread and fish in your hand only to see the same amount still there! Well you know the rest of the story.

So here are the Questions for the Day

Do you see the needs of those around you? Do you see the lost co-workers? Do you see the widow neighbor? Do you see ... ? As you pray for them, asking Jesus do something to meet their needs, do you hear Him say to you, "you do something?" Do you realize that what you have is grossly inadequate to meet the needs? Are you willing to give Jesus your lunch, not just part of your lunch but all of your lunch? The miracle is waiting but will never happen until you give Jesus your lunch. What is Jesus asking you to give Him? What are you holding on to that Jesus is asking you to give?

Jesus wants your lunch.

TO FORGIVE

MATT 6:14–15; MATT 18:22–35

"I hate that person" are words that flowed from my lips with fervent intent. The situation had come to the point that hate had genuinely taken root at the core of my heart towards another. This was not a passing inflamed emotion but an anchored one. I had disliked some people throughout life, but this one I hated. Injury, not once, but repeatedly, had been done to my family and me by this one's actions. Therefore, I felt justified in my hate towards this person.

I knew I wasn't supposed to "hate" anyone, especially ones that were "called" my brother or sister in Christ. Oh, I confronted them about their actions and injury to my family and they apologized. I didn't want their apology I wanted vengeance! Besides, they didn't really seem very sorry for their injurious actions.

IT DOESN'T SEEM FAIR

It just doesn't seem fair; they do the intentional injury, say, "I'm sorry" and go on with life while you're left to pick up the pieces and somehow go on with yours. Therefore, holding on to the hate and un-forgiveness in some warped way makes you think you're getting them back. Actually, they're sleeping pretty good.

If someone has intentionally done you harm do you have to forgive?

> For if you forgive men their trespasses, your heavenly Father will also forgive you. ¹⁵But if you do not forgive men their trespasses, neither will your Father forgive your trespasses.
>
> Matt 6:14–15 (NKJV)

Seems clear, if you don't forgive others then God doesn't forgive you! In fact read Matt 18:22–35. Notice how Jesus ends this story about forgiveness:

> So my heavenly Father also will do to you if each of you, from his heart, does not forgive his brother his trespasses.
>
> Matt 18:35 (NKJV)

THE KEY TO FORGIVENESS

There's the key to forgiveness—"from your heart." I had said, "I forgive them" more than once, but at the thought or mention of their name anger, bitterness, resentment, and alike immediately boiled up within me. There's the test to see if you've truly forgiven them. When you think about them, does anger towards them arise in your heart? If so, you haven't completely forgiven them.

A FAULTY THOUGHT

One of the faulty thought processes about this kind of forgiveness is, "if you forgive them then you are agreeing with what they did was right."

God doesn't agree that our sins are right, yet he forgives us. To release someone from your heart isn't agreeing with them, it's simply releasing them from your anger. Depending on how deep the anger will depend how much you have to release. I can tell you from personal experience the more you take it to God in prayer and bathe yourself in His presence, the more you'll forgive from your heart.

Well, do you have anyone that you need to forgive? Whether they ask for forgiveness or not doesn't matter, you must forgive. Take it to God in prayer, release it to Him, and ask Him to pour healing into your heart.

"For if you forgive men their trespasses, your heavenly Father will also forgive you."

WHAT'S WITH ALL THE GIFTS?

GEN 41:50–52; ROM 8:28–29; PHIL 3:7–11;
GEN 50:19–20

I had had some disturbing dreams the past few nights. In my dreams, I was back at a place where much emotional damage had taken place for me and my family. Much of the insult took place in the room. In my dream, this room was filled from top to bottom and side to side with all kinds of lovely wrapped gifts. In my dream I thought, "wow he sure is being blessed."

It was confusing to me that someone that treats people the way he did would be so blessed by God. I questioned the LORD about this in my prayer times and said, "What's with all the gifts for this guy? "Why are you blessing him so?" The LORD responded, "Those are your gifts." What!? Again I thought God was confused on who He was talking to. How, I questioned, are those my gifts?

IT REMINDED ME OF THE PAIN

In my mind that room, that place, had come to represent such pain and turmoil and every dream that I had had before about this place had always brought feelings of pain and anger. Now that I had truly released my un-forgiveness towards this brother and was ready to get on with life, I have this dream. I questioned God, (something I'm sure you've never done) "God how could this room, this place that in my mind represents such pain, that is now full of gifts, be for me? What good came out of any of that pain, confusion, anger, and bitterness? God reminded me of what Joseph named his children.

> Joseph called the name of the firstborn Manasseh: "For God has made me forget all my toil and all my father's house." ⁵²And the name of the second he called Ephraim: "For God has caused me to be fruitful in the land of my affliction."
>
> Gen 41:51–52 (NKJV)

PRACTICAL APPLICATION

What the devil meant for bad, God was able use it for good. Joseph had learned this so much so that he named his two children to reflect how God used the bad times to bring about good. I have been able to take those painful experiences and use them to minister to others and what a gift it is to be able to do that! The gift is not the pain and suffering but how God brought me through it and the lessons He taught me.

WHAT GIFTS DO YOU HAVE?

What are the hard times has God brought you through? What painful experiences has God brought you through? Are you still trapped in the bitterness? I hope that this gives you a different point of view to trials and tribulations. If you will keep your faith in God, and sometimes that's the hardest thing you'll ever do, God will bring you through it.

> For I know the thoughts that I think toward you, says the LORD, thoughts of peace and not of evil, to give you a future and a hope.
>
> Jer 29:11 (NKJV)

> The Spirit of the LORD God is upon Me, Because the LORD has anointed Me To preach good tidings to the poor; He has sent Me to heal the brokenhearted, To proclaim liberty to the captives, And the opening of the prison to those who are bound; ²To proclaim the acceptable year of the LORD, And the day of vengeance of our God; To comfort all who mourn, ³ To console those who mourn in Zion, To give them beauty for ashes, The oil of joy for mourning, The garment of praise for the spirit of heaviness; That they may be called trees of righteousness, The planting of the LORD, that He may be glorified.
>
> Isa 61:1–3 (NKJV)

CHALLENGE

How are you looking at your past troubles and trials? Are you allowing the devil the pleasure of stealing your gifts? He steals them when we don't use our past hurts, pains, trials, etc., as a gift to use to minister to someone else going through a similar situation. Do you see your past troubles and trials as a gift that can be used for God? If you are still caught in the bitterness, go to Jesus and pour your heart out to Him, pour out all the bitterness and pain. Ask Jesus to show you the lessons and ask Him to help you use them for His glory and to continue to heal any pain that may still be associated with those events.

WHEN THE HEAT IS ON

DANIEL 3

For several months, everyone had not only heard but seen the progress of the statue being built. People knew that it was an idol of the King and he was going to decree that everyone bow down and worship it. Three men, appointed governors by the King, knew that God forbid idol worship. They knew that to bow down would be in direct disobedience to God.

Thousands of people, at the King's decree, had gathered for this event. They were all standing around this massive nine-foot wide, nine-foot thick, ninety-foot tall statue of the King and made of gold no less. A decree was heralded that when the band began to play, everyone was to bow down to the idol in adoration and worship or else they would be thrown in a fiery furnace.

The symphonic band began to play and immediately thousands of people dropped to the ground in submissive adoration to the idol. However, standing in the midst of this sea of submissive adoration were three men, and they would not bow. Word of this reached the King, who was furious and had them brought before him. He had heard that they served only one God and would not bow to him or his gods.

USE YOUR IMAGINATION

Okay, you know the rest of the story, but put yourself in their shoes. You don't know the outcome; you just know that you've been called on the carpet. You're about to be fired (pun intended) if you don't compromise or renounce your faith. You're looking at the fiery furnace, it's real, and it's hot. Why not bow? I mean what harm will it do? It'll save your life (your job).

AN OFFER YOU CAN'T REFUSE

The King had made them an offer he thought they couldn't refuse. However, look at the steadfastness of their faith that was expressed with such boldness.

> ¹⁶Shadrach, Meshach, and Abed-Nego answered and said to the king, "O Nebuchadnezzar, we have no need to answer you in this matter. ¹⁷If that is the case, our God whom we serve is able to deliver us from the burning fiery furnace, and He will deliver us from your hand, O king. ¹⁸But if not, let it be known to you, O king, that we do not serve your gods, nor will we worship the gold image which you have set up."
>
> Daniel 3:16–18 (NKJV)

HOW?

How could they face such heat and not waver in their faith? How can you face the heat and not waver in your faith?

They did and you can *if* you have a made up mind *before* you face the heat. You must settle it now that you will not bow to the pressures of temptation. You will not bow and compromise your faith on the job. You will not participate in activities that you know are unethical. You will not do things that compromise your faith, no matter what the cost.

If you're job is on the line because you refuse to compromise, so be it. If friendships are on the line because you refuse to participate, so be it. If family members ostracize you because of your faith, so be it. Nevertheless, whatever you do settle it right now, before you face the heat that *you will not bow.*

"let it be known to you, O king, that we do not serve your gods, nor will we worship the gold image which you have set up."

BUT IF NOT

DANIEL 3

It was around seven p.m. on a Friday night in the fall when a knock came at the front door. Charles opened the door to see a young man standing there with tears streaming down his face. The young man knew that Charles was a minister but the two had never met. The young man's wife had just packed her bags and left him and he was devastated. He knew he wasn't living right and needed Charles' help to pray him home to God. Charles brought him in and prayed with him. The young man wept and poured his heart out to God. When he was done, he felt like the weight of the world had been lifted from his shoulders.

A PROBING QUESTION

He then asked Charles to pray with him that his wife would come back. "I just know that since I've come back to God He will bring her back to me."

Charles said to the young man, "If not ... then what?"

"If not, are you still going to serve God?" The young

man was startled by the question, had the true motive for his faith been exposed? Was it a faith that would serve God as long as God did what he wanted? The young man managed to say in so many words that he would serve God if his wife didn't come back to him. Within three months, he went back to his old lifestyle because his wife filed for divorce.

A Statement of Faith

The three Hebrew children made a statement that shows how deep their faith and allegiance to God really was. They were facing the most powerful earthly king of their day. He told them to bend, bow, or burn. Their life was on the line. If they didn't do what the King told them to do, they were going to be executed in a very dreadful fashion. Because their mind was made up before they faced the trial, they didn't hesitate in their answer to him.

> Shadrach, Meshach, and Abed-Nego answered and said to the king, "O Nebuchadnezzar, we have no need to answer you in this matter. ¹⁷If that is the case, our God whom we serve is able to deliver us from the burning fiery furnace, and He will deliver us from your hand, O king.
>
> Dan 3:16–17 (NKJV)

Wow what a confident statement and a statement that many Christian's have made. "God is able," "He will come through for me," "He will not let me suffer," "He will deliver me."…Oh you can really stir up a Church crowd up with talk like that! However, these guys went on in their statement to a place that many Christians do not go. They said, "but if not."

What Did They Say?

Hey whoa here, what did they say? Did they say "but if not?" That's where many hyper-faith Christians would part ways. The three Hebrew children were speaking doubt into the situation by saying, "but if not." Actually, they were making the greatest faith statement a Christian can ever make. I will serve God even if He doesn't deliver me. Even if the flames of your kingly wrath torment us until we die, we will die for our faith in God. Now that's a faith statement. That's faith that is rooted and grounded in serving God for *who* He is and not *what* He does for us.

What's Your Faith Statement?

So what's your faith grounded upon? Do you have faith in God because of *what* He does for you or is your faith ground in God for *who* He is? Notice that as they were bound and being carried to the fiery furnace, they didn't whine to God about being thrown into the fire. They simply held their faith in silent confidence that no matter what, they would serve the LORD.

Can you make a "but if not" statement of faith?

[18]*But if not, let it be known to you, O king, that we do not serve your gods, nor will we worship the gold image which you have set up."*

Your Fiery Furnace Awaits

Daniel 3

The executioner took a rope and bound Shadrach from his shoulders down to his ankles so that he couldn't move. Then a very strong soldier picked him up over his head and began walking Shadrach towards his fate, a fiery furnace. Thoughts raced through his mind as he resolved himself to his fate.

Thoughts of a Challenging Life

Shadrach's life had been filled with so many challenges. He remembered the day when Babylonian soldiers charged into his house and took him away from his parents. He was a teenager at the time and had not seen his parents since that day. The last images of his parents was that of his father holding his mother as she tearfully pleaded that they would not take him away. He could still hear the agony of her cries. Many days he thought about them and what had became of them but he just didn't know.

From there he was placed in the Kings "re-education"

program to train him to be a government official, an official of the very government that caused the separation of his family. There were many "cut-throat" people in this school that had maligned his reputation to get "ahead" politically. That maligning didn't stop once he graduated but continued all along. In fact, that was one of the reasons he was being lead away to his fate.

His Greatest Challenges

However, the greatest challenges Shadrach faced were spiritual ones. All around him was the sinful decadence of a pagan society that was constantly pulling at him, but he had remained faithful to God. That faithfulness was leading him to the executioner's fire.

He could hear the jeers of the crowd as they drew closer to the fiery furnace. Shadrach closed his eyes as he felt the increasing heat. The strong man carrying him began to stumble as the heat of the furnace was taking its toll. With every last ounce of strength, the strong man heaved Shadrach into the fiery furnace.

The Pain of Fire

Shadrach grimaced expecting the searing pain of the fire to seize his body. As he hit the floor of the furnace, he felt the ropes release his body. Still expecting the pain, he felt nothing. He opened his eyes to see the bodies of his two friends Meshach and Abed-Nego hit the furnace floor and watched a blaze of fire engulf the ropes that had bound them. Shadrach wondered if he couldn't feel the pain because he was dead. He stood up and walked over to his friends, who by this time were gathering their wits as well. He reached out his hands to them to lift them up. When they took Shadrach by the hand, it proved they were not dead. They began walking around in the fire praising God for his mighty power. It wasn't long before they heard the voice of the King calling unto them to come out of the fire.

Reality Is

You know the rest of the story. I just wanted to put you in the story to remember that Shadrach was a real person with real emotions and struggles just like you. Are we not surrounded by a decadent society that constantly pulls at us to follow them into sin? Do we not face the challenges of the work place from time to time? Do we not receive threats in so many words or ways to bend, bow, or burn?

Your Fiery Furnace Awaits!

Are you being readied for the fiery furnace? Are you in the fiery furnace? Take heart and stand firm for Jesus, because that's what He did for you at the cross. He will never leave you nor forsake you but will always be with you. Make up your mind now, before you face the fiery furnace, that you will *not* bow and it will be easier when the heat is on.

Never Alone

We don't know if Shadrach and his friends could see Jesus walking in the fire with them. We know from the testimony of the King that Jesus was there walking with them. Know this, if you stand up for Jesus He will stand with you in the fire. Also, notice that the very thing that the devil devised to destroy Shadrach and his friends is the very thing God used to deliver them.

"Look!" he answered, "I see four men loose, walking in the midst of the fire; and they are not hurt, and the form of the fourth is like the Son of God."

INTO THE STORM
MARK 6:45–51; DEUT 8:2; PROV 3:5–6

The weather turned foul quickly and unexpectedly. The boat was being swamped from the waves that were crashing over the bow of the boat. All energy and focus was on staying alive. To make matters worse, it was in the middle of the night, so darkness took on a whole new meaning. The men in this boat were thinking of death because the circumstances were that grave. I'm sure that some of those men were thinking, "Why did He send us out here if He knew we would face this storm? Why is He not in the boat with us? Why are we all alone?"

JESUS SENT THEM

Jesus sent his disciples out in the boat *knowing* that they would be caught in a storm in the middle of the night. The question is, why? If He loved us, wouldn't He keep us from facing these storms?

First, I can assure you that there are many, many storms that God keeps us from that the world faces everyday.

Sometimes the devil brings storms to buffet and discourage you. Know this, God never leads you somewhere without a purpose and yes, sometimes God even leads you directly into the path of a storm. But why does He do that? God does that to build us up never to destroy us.

WHEN THE HEAT IS ON

God led the Children of Israel out of Egypt and into the wilderness to test them and show them what was in their hearts. What is truly in your heart will surface when the heat is on. God already knows what's in your heart, but you don't. Therefore, He purposely, for your own good, will allow or take you into the storm.

> "The heart is deceitful above all things, And desperately wicked; Who can know it? I, the LORD, search the heart, I test the mind, Even to give every man according to his ways, According to the fruit of his doings.
>
> Jer 17:9–10 (NKJV)

WHEN THE STORM COMES

Therefore, in the storms of life you need to ask God in prayer to give you wisdom for the reason of the storm. Is it a test? What is He trying to show you and teach you? Is it ordained by Him or is it from the devil? Even if it is brought on by the devil, it is still a test that God will use for His glory.

Know this, throughout the Bible from Geneses to Revelations, every storm that God's children faced, *if they held firm to Him*, He always brought them through!

I'll leave you with these verses of scripture because the Word of God builds your faith. The storm will *not* destroy you *if* you will stand firm and have faith in God.

The steps of a good man are ordered by the LORD, And He delights in his way. Though he fall, he shall not be utterly cast down; For the LORD upholds him with His hand. I have been young, and now am old; Yet I have not seen the righteous forsaken, Nor his descendants begging bread. He is ever merciful, and lends; And his descendants are blessed.

Psa 37:23–26 (NKJV)

Fear not, for I am with you; Be not dismayed, for I am your God. I will strengthen you, Yes, I will help you, I will uphold you with My righteous right hand. Behold, all those who were incensed against you Shall be ashamed and disgraced; They shall be as nothing, And those who strive with you shall perish.

Isa 41:10–11 (NKJV)

But now, thus says the LORD, who created you, O Jacob, And He who formed you, O Israel: "Fear not, for I have redeemed you; I have called you by your name; You are Mine. When you pass through the waters, I will be with you; And through the rivers, they shall not overflow you. When you walk through the fire, you shall not be burned, Nor shall the flame scorch you.

Isa 43:1–2 (NKJV)

The LORD is on my side; I will not fear. What can man do to me?

Psa 118:6 (NKJV)

No weapon formed against you shall prosper, And every tongue which rises against you in judgment You shall condemn. This is the heritage of the servants of the LORD, And their righteousness is from Me," Says the LORD.

Isa 54:17 (NKJV)

Yea, though I walk through the valley of the shadow of death, I will fear no evil; For You are with me; Your rod and Your staff, they comfort me.

Psa 23:4 (NKJV)

A LOVE THAT LASTS

1 COR 13:4–8

The ushers had seated all of the guests. The groom and groomsman were in their places. The cute little ring bearer and flower girl had paraded down the aisle to the chuckles of the guest. Then there came the crescendo of the Bride's stanza, that alerted all present that the bride was entering the ceremony. The crowd stood to their feet and everyone was trying to catch that first glimpse of the bride as she came down the aisle.

On their wedding day, the young couple, all wrapped up in "love," made some commitments through vows that they would love each other until the day they died. Only they didn't die, they got a divorce. With the divorce rate in our society at 50% plus, of which is the same for those who say they are "Christians," is there any such thing as a love that lasts? Okay I know that there are some who are reading this that have been divorced and remarried but stay with me.

WRONG DEFINITION

Our society has confused *lust* with *love*. That confusion has made its way into the church. Lust is *based* upon "emotions" and emotions come and go. Ok so what about "Christians" who marry and divorce? Did they get love and lust confused? Perhaps to some degree, so allow me to explain.

SO WHAT IS LOVE?

In the New Testament, there are two Greek words that are translated in English as "love," but their *foundations* are completely different. One is *phileo, which* is *based* more on emotional attachment or emotions of affection. The other word is *agape* which is *based* first upon a choice of your will. *Agape* is *not* void of emotions it's just *not* the foundation of it.

The most famous verse in the Bible John 3:16, "for God so loved (*agape*) the world," shows that God's love is a love based upon the choice of His will.

CONTINUE TO MAKE THE RIGHT CHOICE

Sometimes I don't *feel* in love with my wife so I must *choose* to love her. Of course, sometimes she doesn't *feel* in love with me either! Therefore, we must constantly *choose* to love each other, because if one of us or both of us ever stop choosing to love the other then our marriage will eventually fail.

That holds true in my relationship with God. Will I love Him when I don't "feel" His presence? Will I love Him when I don't "see" what I want to see working in my life? I must settle in my heart that God has chosen to love me and He will not change His choice.

THE PAST AND NOW THE PRESENT

I know there are those reading this that were married and were truly in love with each other, unfortunately one chose to stop loving the other, which lead to a divorce. My prayer is that God will heal your broken heart and that in your current marriage both parties will continue to chose to love each other.

Ultimately, we cannot make anyone love us, but we can help the process towards that end. How? Read 1 Cor 13:4–8a and that will show you what love *(agape)* is and how it behaves, which is how you should be and behave. Bottom line is, do not let emotions rule your love, but let true love rule your emotions. Love never fails.

A GOOD THING

GEN 2:18–23; PROV 18:22; PS 37:23;
PROV 3:5–6

DISCLAIMER!

Okay today's devotional is going to be a bit different and one of a kind. Guys probably won't get much out of this one (but they should), but the ladies might because it's a love story.

FISH IN THE SEA

As a teenager, one of my primary concerns was finding that one girl that would be my wife. Many times, I prayed that the rapture would not take place until I was married. (Oh, you can relate too?) The closer I got to being a senior in high school the more concerned I became about having that Mrs. Right. Without going into the soap opera story of my dating life, let me just say I graduated from high school without any prospects. I had just left the largest concentration of prospects *(fish in the sea)* when I graduated. Of course, my number one requirement was that they be a Christian.

God said that He directs our steps. So I settled the issue in my heart to give it to God and let Him bring that special one into my life when He pleased. It was one of the hardest things I've ever done because many of my friends were already paired off.

SUNDAY, NOVEMBER 13, 1983.

After church, some friends and I were talking about where to go to eat. We said "Pizza Hut," but when we looked in our wallets we said, "McDonald's." A young lady and her friends left from another church heading to Pizza Hut. For some reason during the drive, they decided to drive by McD's to see "what was going on." After they circled a couple of times, they decided to stop at McD's.

GOD DIRECTS OUR PATHS

Let me show you how God works in our destiny. This young lady had previously lived in Indiana and I lived in Florida. Between her junior and senior year of high school she had the opportunity to move to my town and live with her older sister. In doing so, she would have attended my high school and would have been in my senior class, of which I would have met her then. She decided not to move.

After her graduation, she moved to my town to live with her sister. Her church didn't have a youth group so one night she visited my youth group. I had probably only missed one in a thousand youth services and the one I missed was the one that she visited. Two separate and distinct times our paths would have crossed but they didn't

PATHS OF DESTINY

I was sitting with my friends at McD's and literally, when this young lady walked through the door, my eyes met hers and I was immediately captivated by those beautiful brown eyes and her smile. It melted my heart. Unbeknownst to me, she naturally was and still is a shy person. Her friends encouraged her to come over to my table and introduce herself because she had recognized my friends from when she visited our youth group.

That night changed my life and began a two and half year journey leading to my wedding day, May 24, 1986. Shawn became my wife that day and I loved her more than I loved any woman. I didn't think it possible to love her any deeper than I did that day. I was wrong. I love her more today than I did over twenty-one years ago.

> He who finds a wife finds a good thing, And obtains favor from the Lord.
>
> Prov 18:22 (NKJV)

I have obtained great favor from the Lord! Oh, we've had our ups and downs in our marriage, wars and rumors of wars. But at the end of those wars, we find our relationship growing stronger, because we choose to love one another and choose to cherish our marriage.

By now, my wife reading this is embarrassed to death. I just wanted to celebrate the institution of marriage and testify that I have a good thing and God has greatly blessed me!

> He who finds a wife finds a good thing, And obtains favor from the Lord.
>
> Prov 18:22 (NKJV)

Shawn, you are my good thing and thanks for choosing to be my wife. I love you F.E.M.

How To Get Ready
For Church–Part 1

I was glad when they said to me, "Let us go into the house of the Lord."

Psa 122:1 (NKJV)

The beeping of the alarm clock breaks the silence of the morning. With contempt, the alarm is forced into submission by pushing the snooze button. This tussle goes back and forth for the next thirty minutes. Finally, the snoozer surrenders to the alarm clock. Squinting to focus through bleary eyes, he realizes the time, 9:30. "9:30," he exclaims, which causes his wife to shoot up out of bed. "9:30! We are going to be late, again!" she says.

All Hands on Deck

Like a Navy ship going into "all hands on deck" mode, they roused the family from their slumber.

Moans and groans could be heard from the teen's room as

dad barged in with the "all hands on deck" command. "Come on, lets go, everybody out of bed it's church day," said dad.

"Ah dad, just a few more minutes," they moaned, "we didn't get in from the movies until 1 a.m. We had to have something to eat because were hungry and then had to watch a bit of TV to unwind, so we didn't get in bed until three a.m."

"Well I'm telling you to get up," said dad, "so lets go." He exited their room and headed to the kitchen. The kids just moaned and rolled over in the bed, not phased by the command of the "captain."

A Relaxing Morning

Dad makes a pot of coffee, retrieves the morning paper and sits at the table to get caught up on the sports scores. A few minutes later, mom, the "admiral," enters the kitchen, "Where are the kids?" Dad, the captain, shrugs his shoulders and says, "I told them to get out of bed."

"Well obviously they didn't listen to you now did they?," and off she storms to the kids room.

The admiral was definitely heard. Who couldn't hear it? The neighbors were roused out of bed from her commands. "I said get out of bed! Don't you roll those eyes at me young man, I'll roll them right out of your head! Now get up and I mean *now*!" She stormed out of their room, slamming the door behind her.

What Were We Talking About?

She entered the kitchen, "Well are you going to sit there all morning or do something to help me?" "I'm catching up on all the sports scores," he defended.

"Sports, smorts ... Why are we paying for that high priced two zillion sports ticket digital satellite for?" she barked.

"So I can watch the games," he sarcastically barked back.

"They don't tell you the score, you have to pay extra and buy the newspaper?" she rebuffed.

"Hey don't criticize me; you're the one that watches all those shopping channels running up the credit card bill. Then on Saturday morning you scour the classifies for yard sales and run all over town in your five miles to the gallon SUV and buy peoples junk, which you haul to the $70 a month storage shed!"

"What does that have to do with getting ready for church?" she demanded.

"Fine, I'll get ready for church, admiral," he smirked.

KIDS

As dad was storming out, the kids were dragging in. Sitting at the table with cereal in hand, they began to fight over the comics. As they tugged and tussled over the comics, one of them let go on purpose to cause the other one to lose their balance and it worked, except that it caused cereal to go flying all over the kitchen.

The admiral went through the roof! "Dad burn it! You guys clean that mess up right now! You guys are going to cause us to be late for church!"

"Well he started it," complained one of the siblings.

"Well, I don't care who started it, you're both going to clean it up and clean it up now!"

"I've got to go get ready for church," she said as she huffed out of the kitchen.

THE JOYFUL RIDE TO CHURCH

At 10:25, fighting like the Hatfield's and the McCoy's, they loaded into the car. All the way to church there were aggravated verbal volleys tossed back and forth. As they pulled into the church parking lot dad growled, "Well we're late again! Why do we come to church if we're going to be late every week," he demanded without really expecting an answer.

Entering His Gates with Thanksgiving

As they entered the foyer, smiling greeters greeted them. "Good morning," said one of the greeters with a genuine smile and a robust handshake. The family squeezed out a semi sarcastic smile.

"We trust that you'll enjoy the peace and presence of the Lord today," the other greeted said.

The mom rolled her eyes at the family, "Peace, well that's a new concept on Sunday mornings for our family," she mumbled under her breath.

They entered the sanctuary with the worship service already in progress. "Well all the Christians got here before us; all the back seats are taken," said dad.

"Why do we have to stand so long anyway," he thought as they made their way towards the front of the seating area.

Later, as the pastor took the pulpit to bring the message, dad thought to himself, "I hope the preacher doesn't go past twelve today. There's a good game coming on at one and we've got to beat the other church to the buffet line or I'll miss the first quarter of the game." The kids just slouched down in their seats to rest their heads on the back of the chair to catch a nap. Mom was digging in her purse trying to find that shopping list to add a few things she'd thought of.

How Do You Get Ready For Church?

So how do you get ready for church? Does this painfully sound a bit like your family? In the next chapter, we will look at how to get ready for church.

> *I was glad when they said to me, "Let us go into the house of the* Lord. *"*
>
> Psa 122:1 (NKJV)

How To Get Ready
for Church–Part 2

I was glad when they said to me, Let us go into the house of the Lord."

Psa 122:1 (NKJV)

I imagine in the previous chapter together, that the fictitious story may have had some painful truth that hit home for you. What is it like at your house on Sunday morning getting ready for church? Are you flabbergasted by the time you pull into the church parking lot? No wonder so much energy and effort is put into the Sunday worship service to get "Christians" energized for another week. From the heating and cooling, the ambiance, the music, the visual, the preaching, etc, many times there is an enormous amount of energy expelled just to get a simple spark in the worship service.

The Problem

For the most part, the problem is we do not know how or when to get ready for church. I am not talking about getting to bed earlier Saturday night and getting up earlier on Sunday morning. Nor am I talking about what to wear, although those things do play a part. What I am talking about getting yourself, you, who you are on the inside, your spirit-man, ready for church.

When to Get Ready For Church

You start getting ready for Sunday worship service on Monday morning. Do you have a regular devotional time throughout the week? Do you have a consistent prayer life throughout the week? Do you listen to praise and worship music throughout the week? If not, then on Sunday morning, you will not be ready for church, regardless of what you wear or what time you arrive at church. If you are getting ready each day of the week, then on Sunday, when we collectively come to the worship service, you will be ready for church.

Easy Solution–Hard To Implement

That is an easy solution but seemingly hard to implement because life is so hectic. Sunday morning is probably a reflection of every morning. We are a pushed and driven society. We are pushed to be more productive on the job and in our personal life. With the advent of "email" and "cell phones," we are more distracted than ever before while on the job and in our personal lives. "Email" and "cell phones," are not the problem but how we allow them to rule our life could be.

"You've Got Mail"

The bottom line is we are such a distracted society that we are missing spending time with God. Oh I have heard the excuses from guys, "When I am out in nature I feel close to God," which would be a true statement if that was your sole purpose of being out in nature, rather than a sporting event. I have never heard a woman say, "When I'm shopping I feel so close to God." Anyway, you are just going to have to take the time to get ready for church by stealing away with God in prayer and His Word.

ARE READY FOR CHURCH?

> *I was glad when they said to me, Let us go into the house of the* LORD.*"*

Psa 122:1 (NKJV)

TRUST THE INSTRUMENTS

PROV 3:5–7

THE PERFECT STORM

His mind raced with thoughts of his family and if he would ever see them again. He had been in many storms before but none this fierce before. He was an experienced pilot with hundreds of hours logged as a pilot. He was very studious in pilot's manuals as well, but neither his experience nor studies prepared him for the real experience of a storm of this magnitude. The plane shuttered and weaved to and fro, and the sound of the rain beating against the windshield was nothing less than deafening. He was struggling to keep the plane in any semblance of control.

A GREATER DILEMMA

He knew that if he was going to make it he had to pull up out of the storm, but a greater dilemma now confronted him. His senses told him that he was right side up, but his flight instruments said he was flying upside down. His senses told him that he was close to the top of storm, several thousand feet in the air, but his instruments said he was just 2,000 feet above the ground.

If he went with his senses and pulled up and they were wrong he would come out of the storm heading to the ground and would not have enough time to turn the plane right side up and avert disaster. He sat there in his cockpit, alone, frightened, and wondering if he should go with his senses or with the flight instruments.

Spiritual Vertigo

What this pilot was experiencing is what many call "vertigo," which is when your senses are all confused and you don't know which way is up. In this life, we can get caught up in some nasty storms and many times, we get "spiritual vertigo." Our senses tell us one thing but the Word of God tells us something else. So what are you to do? Do you go with your senses or trust the Bible?

Well it would seem that the answer is obvious, but even though the Word of God is absolutely trustworthy there are many "Christians" who fail to trust the instrument and go with their senses only to pull out of the storm heading towards disaster.

Trust the Instrument

Trust the true instrument of life; trust the Word of God. Perhaps you are experiencing "spiritual vertigo" and your surroundings tell you one thing but God's Word tells you another. You cannot see how God's Word could be right in this situation but trust your instruments!

> Heaven and earth will pass away, but My words will by no means pass away.
>
> Luke 21:33 (NKJV)

Do you trust the instrument? How you live your life shows if you really do or not.

I Wish I Hadn't Done That

JOHN 8:3–12; LUKE 15:11–31; 1 JOHN 1:6–2:2;
ROM 8:1–16

She lay there in the dust with a circle of shadows crowding around her, angry, mean, vindictive shadows. These were the shadows of her past that had finally caught up with her. Just moments before, she was living her life without much regret or at least not enough to cause her to change. Now she lay in the dust, fearing the judgment that these shadows would bring. As she hears their taunts of judgment, her mind begins to fill with thoughts of regret.

The fun she had been having, she now realizes, was just a deceptive cover up to ease the pain of her regrets. She knew that what she was doing was wrong, but she kept doing it anyway. The fun only lasted for a moment and then she was left to her thoughts of regret. There were so many things that she wished she hadn't done but to no avail, they had been done and now she must face the consequences of her actions.

Those angry shadows closed in, demanding judgment be cast upon her for her sins. She did not and could not deny the truth of the testimony those shadows uttered. Tears began to roll down her face making streaks as each tear washed away a bit of the dust of shame. Oh how regrets consumed her! The thoughts of "Oh I wished I hadn't done that!" The thoughts of "if only."

In the midst of those shadows of judgment, there appeared another shadow, a shadow that brought peace to the air of confusion. It was the shadow of mercy and grace. This shadow realized that she was regretfully repentant. This shadow brought no words of judgment, condemnation, or regrets only words of mercy, grace, and forgiveness with a charge to go and sin no more.

I WISH I HADN'T DONE THAT...

...are words that I am sure all of us have uttered at some point in our life. We all have regrets and some regrets are bigger, much bigger than others. Do you have any regrets that still weigh heavy on your soul even after many years? Have you gone to Jesus time and time again asking for forgiveness and even though you have not done that regrettable deed again, you still feel its weight? If so, I can relate.

The struggle comes from not fully understanding God's grace. Yeah, none of us deserve anything from God, that's a given, but the fact is He has given us much. It has been said that "mercy" is withholding what we truly deserved and that is "judgment." "Grace" is giving us what we do not deserve, all the riches of Christ. You have been restored to the Family of God, receiving all the authority that comes from being a child of God! Just like the prodigal Luke 15:11ff.

Imagine what that woman lying in the dust at the feet of Jesus experienced. Expecting condemnation, judgment, and death, He lifted her up out of the dust, forgave her and challenged her to go and sin no more. I'm sure that in the days that followed those same old regrets once again begin to weight heavy on her soul. Can you relate? What do we do with those regrets that we have truly repented and ask Jesus to forgive us of?

USE REGRETS FOR POSITIVE

Well regrets can be used in a positive way. They can help keep you from making those mistakes again. They can be used to warn others from making those mistakes. They can be used as a testimony of God's mercy and grace.

THE APOSTLE PAUL HAD SOME REGRETS

However, Paul used those in a positive way to testify of God's mercy and grace. He also used them to spur him on to pursue the things of God. Phil 3:1–14; 1 Tim 1:12–17

If those thoughts of forgiven regrets bring you down and you keep reliving the pain of those regrets, that's condemnation. Condemnation only comes from one place, the devil. Romans 8:1–17 clearly shows that if you are *not* pursuing those fleshly appetites, but actively pursuing obedience to the things of God then you should have no fear of those thoughts of past sins.

CONVICTION VERSES CONDEMNATION?

Conviction and condemnation have one element that is the same and that is "guilt." The difference between them though is vast. Condemnation is guilt without hope of remedying that guilt. Conviction is guilt with hope, hope of deliverance and forgiveness. The devil brings condemnation but the Holy Spirit brings conviction.

YOUR REGRETS

Are you struggling with the weight of regrets? Have you asked Jesus to forgive you? Have you stopped that which brought you regret? If you answered yes to all three of those questions then you need to ask God to help you understand the greatness of His grace, not in a cognitive way but in an experiential way. Paul prayed this for all believers. Phil 3:14–19

If you are caught up in regrets and those regrets keep leading you to sin and more regrets cry out to Jesus to save you! You might also consider that which I encouraged in another devotional *"The Haunted House."*

> Confess your trespasses to one another, and pray
> for one another, that you may be healed …
>
> James 5:16 (NKJV)

You need a trusted Christian, which could be your spouse, a friend, anyone that you can really trust. Tell them of the struggle you are having and that you need them to help you. First thing they can do to help you is not tell others about this struggle. The second thing they can do is ask you the tough questions. The third thing they can do is pray for you and with you.

The Secret Place

Psa 91

When Dorothy was 7 years old, she discovered a secret room behind the bookcase in the study of the house they had recently moved into. It was a small little room that was lit with natural light. She didn't tell her parents about it because she wanted it to be her little secret. She would steal away to this secret place quite often and take her dollies and have wonderful tea parties and alike. She felt so safe in this little secret place.

Thieves Broke In

One afternoon when she was home alone, some evil men broke into the house. Dorothy immediately ran to her secret place. Once in her secret place she could hear the men rummaging through the house but knew that they would never find her and they didn't. She stayed in there until she heard the voice of her parents calling out to her. They were shocked to see the bookcase swing open and their precious little daughter come bounding out unharmed and undaunted by all that had happened.

Oh To Have A Secret Place

Wouldn't it be wonderful if there were a secret place where you could go to hide from the enemy of your soul? A secret place where the devil's presence of fear could not reach you, a place where his voice of doubt could not be heard, a place where he could not find you no matter how hard he tried. Well, there is such a place; it is the presence of God.

Notice what verse one of Psalm 91 states: "He that dwells." The secret to this place is dwelling. Do you dwell there or do you pass by on your way to a busy life? I ask you to read Psalm 91 entirely. Verse one gives the condition for the benefits of verses 3–13. In verses 14–16 God Himself is declaring what He will do for those who dwell in His presence.

Access Granted

The blood of Jesus Christ has given all who will repent of their sins access to God's presence. If you have known sin in your life when you attempt dwell in His presence, the Holy Spirit will deal with you about your sin. If you want to dwell there, you must deal with any sin(s) that His presence reveals in your life.

How does one "dwell" there and still live life?

I mean, unless one becomes a monk and lives in a monastery how can you "dwell" in His presence? It starts by spending some "quiet" time with the LORD, but then you walk in His presence throughout the day. How do you do that? By thinking about Him, communing with Him through your spirit, and by simply obeying His Word as you live the day.

He who dwells in the secret place of the Most High Shall abide under the shadow of the Almighty.

ACCESS GRANTED

MATT 27:50–51; EPH 3:11–12; HEB 4:14–16; HEB 10:19–22

BACKSTAGE PASS

Joe had been given a "backstage" pass from his friend who was going to be performing in town at the civic center. Joe's friend was a very popular singer and was touring the country to sell out audiences at every stop. When Joe arrived at the civic center, it was packed to overflowing. He walked nervously down the side aisle to the area that led behind the stage. At that entranceway was a large, burly, mean looking man dressed in black with white words across his rippling chest muscle spelling "security." As Joe approached this mean looking security guard, he held out his backstage pass. Upon seeing Joe's pass, the security guard smiled and stepped aside for Joe to enter the backstage to see his friend.

ACCESS DENIED

For over 1,200 years, the direct presence of God had been closed access. Only one person had access to the direct presence of God and then he only had access once a year for a few hours. To block this access there was a heavy, thick veil. That veil stood as not only a security guard but as a reminder that humanity no longer had access to God's presence because of their sins. That is not the way God wanted it, so He sent His son to die on the cross to grant us direct access to His presence once again.

ACCESS GRANTED

When Jesus cried aloud on the cross "it is finished," the veil in the Temple, that for years stood to block access, was ripped from top to bottom signifying that if you have a "backstage pass" you can have access to His presence. That pass is faith in Christ for salvation.

Don't lay aside your access pass. Take care that you do not stain it with sin, but if you do have Jesus wash it in His blood. Don't tear it with unforgiveness and bitterness. Take advantage of your granted access because it cost God everything to give you this access.

THE FINAL LAP

HEB 12:1–2

THE FINISH LINE

She knew she was approaching the finish line. Everything within her wanted to give up, yet there was the urge to hang on. It had been a long race with many unexpected obstacles along the way. Yet there had also been many unexpected bursts of energy to overcome those obstacles along the way.

What happens when you take that last breath of air in this life and you cross over the threshold of eternity? We've all heard the stories of the "great tunnel of light." I've heard all kinds of near death and death experiences. I've heard the hell experiences and the heaven experiences.

GREAT CLOUD OF WITNESSES

In Acts 7 when Stephen was being stoned to death, he looked up and saw the heavens opened and Jesus standing at the right hand of God. Jesus was welcoming Stephen into heaven. I have a vivid imagination, so bear with me on this.

This "great cloud of witnesses" are all those who have gone on before us and crossed the finish line. They stand as a testimony that faith in Christ will carry you through anything, all the way into eternity.

THE GRANDSTANDS ERUPT

I imagine (although not scriptural) in heaven there's a great arena, like the ones you see in the Olympics for track and field events. As the runners enter the arena to take their final lap of the 25k race, the stands erupt with deafening cheers. As the runner hears the roar of those cheers, he gets a rush of adrenaline and a surge of power lunges him forward. Every muscle in this body feels no pain. The harshness of the previous 25k is obliterated from his mind. His eyes and mind are fixed upon only one thing, the finish line.

THE FINAL LAP

Using that imagery and that of Heb 12:1–2, here's what I picture. As a child of God takes their last breath in this life, they enter that great tunnel of light. As they near the end of that tunnel, they begin to hear the grandstands of heaven erupt with a roar of cheers. Those grandstands are filled with those of the great cloud of witnesses. They are cheering on this child of God as they come into the arena of heaven for their final lap to the finish line. They look towards the finish line and they see Jesus standing there cheering them on as well. Hearing the roar of this great cloud of witnesses and seeing Jesus, they feel a rush of spiritual energy propelling them forward. They cross the finish line into the awaiting arms of Jesus! *Wow!*

RUN YOUR RACE AND RUN IT WELL

For the rest of us still in the race of life, lay aside all those weights and sins and keep your eyes fixed on the finish line. Keep them especially fixed on the One standing at the finish line cheering you on. Keep your faith solid in Christ and one day as you enter the arena of heaven for the final lap, you too will hear the roar of those witnesses and cross the finish line into the awaiting arms of Jesus.

This devotional was written as a tribute to all those that I know that are now a part of that great cloud of witnesses.

WHAT IS A CHRISTIAN? —PART 1

JOHN 3:16/ ACTS 16:28–31

A CHRISTIAN NATION?

The United States of America claims to be a Christian nation. In survey after survey, the majority of Americans claim they are Christian. Yet when you look at the conscience of America it is any thing but Christian. You can pass out condoms at public high schools, but you cannot pass out the Bible. Over a million babies aborted each year, porn is a multibillion-dollar industry, prime time television shows glorify sexual immorality, homosexuality, lying, cheating, stealing, etc. Yet America is a "Christian" nation? How can the majority of Americans claim to be "Christian" and the majority of them participate in all the immorality?

WHAT IS A CHRISTIAN?

The problem lies in what I see is our society's current definition of "Christian." One popular definition I see is based upon how good I am compared to how bad someone else is. This definition also says: "I am good because I do good works and therefore I am okay with God."

Probably the second most popular definition I see is "I believe in Jesus and therefore I am a Christian."

This definition that I see says, "I have a cognitive knowledge and acknowledge that:

1. Jesus really existed
2. Jesus really died for the sins of the world
3. Jesus really arose from the grave and is now in heaven.

Therefore because I have this cognitive knowledge and acknowledge these things to be true I am a Christian."

The blame for our society in believing in this definition is not with Hollywood or the media. The blame lies at the feet of the church for allowing this definition to go virtually unchallenged in our society both in the Church's declaration and in its conduct.

The doctrine of the church is not a doctrine of perfection! It is a doctrine of mercy, grace, forgiveness, and change!

THE CONFUSION

It appears that the confusion comes from the misinterpretation of the word "believes" in John 3:16. This word "believes" goes way beyond "cognitive" knowledge or "cognitive" acknowledgement. To understand what the word "believes" really means, you have to look at the Bible's definition of what a Christian really is.

WHAT IS THE BIBLICAL DEFINITION OF A CHRISTIAN?

Becoming a Christian, according to the New Testament, is a definite act with significant results.

To see how the Bible defines what a Christian is, we need to look at the message of Christ and the message of the church in the Bible. That is where we will pick up in tomorrow's devotional. If you want ahead, start read the following Scriptures.

Isa 64:6; Luke 13:1–5; John 3:3–5; Matt 4:17; Mark 2:17; Luke 24:46–47; Acts 2:37–38; Acts 3:19; Acts 17:30; Acts 20:19–21; Acts 26:19–20; 2 Cor 7:10; 2 Cor 6:16–18. When you read these Scriptures see if you can see a common theme emerge.

ARE YOU A CHRISTIAN?

Are you a Biblical defined Christian or a society defined Christian? You must be a Biblical defined Christian if you are going to make heaven your home. I will say that it is very appealing to the fleshly nature to be a "society Christian" because there's no real call for real change. However, being a Biblical Christian requires change and complete surrender to the LORDship of Christ. Are you a Christian?

WHAT IS A CHRISTIAN? -PART 2

JOHN 3:16/ ACTS 16:28-31

We are answering the question of what is the Biblical definition of a Christian. Our society has two prevalent definitions. One being that because they are not as bad as someone else, they are a Christian and/or because they do good
works they are acceptable to God.

The second is that because they have a mental acknowledgement that Jesus really existed, died for our sins, and
arose from the grave, they are a Christian. Yet there is no
change in their lives. They continue in what the Bible calls
sin yet believe and declare they are a Christian.

MOST DANGEROUS

This second definition is what I believe to be the most dangerous. This comes from a misinterpretation of the word
"believes" in John 3:16. The word "believes" means much
more than a "mental" or "cognitive" knowledge of Jesus.

The Message of Jesus and the New Testament

To really understand what it means to "believe" in Jesus and through that belief you are a Christian, we must look at the message of Jesus and the New Testament.

If you read the Scriptures from yesterday's devotionals, you will see that the message of Christ and the New Testament differs from our current culture's definition of "believes." Becoming a Christian, according to the New Testament, is a definite act with significant results. In other words, if you "believe" in Jesus there will be a change in your life. That change is being "born again."

How is One "Born Again"?

You have to believe in Jesus.

If you really believe that He died for the sins of the world then you must believe that He died specifically for your sins!

If you really believe that then it will lead you to confess your sins to Christ and repent of your sins because you realize you cannot be good enough in your own works to be acceptable!

Repentance was the Message of Jesus and the Apostles

Repentance is not a common word in our modern vernacular. So what is repentance? It means you change your mind in that you acknowledge that sin is sin and you are sorry for your sins. That sorrow leads you to ask Jesus to forgive you of your sins and starting at that moment, you commit yourself to stop doing sin and start obeying God's Word! In the Bible to be sorry for sins is something that is felt from the core of your heart.

For godly sorrow produces repentance leading to salvation, not to be regretted; but the sorrow of the world produces death.

2 Cor 7:10 (NKJV)

Being "born again" is when the Holy Spirit comes inside of you and births your spirit into life. Being born again means you are no longer the same! (See Rom 6:1–23, 2 Cor 6:16–18)

Being born again doesn't mean that you are perfect or that you will never sin again. What it does mean is that you are striving to serve God through *relational* obedience.

ANOTHER QUESTION

The message of Jesus and the New Testament is a lot different from the current popular definitions of what a Christian is. I asked and answered the question "what is a Christian." I ask you, are you a "Christian"?

Scars

Isa 61:1–3

The knife slipped and sunk deep into the webbing of his hand between the thumb and index finger. The shock of the sight and the registering of immediate pain can still be remembered over thirty years later. Yet he cannot feel the pain anymore, only the remembrance that there was pain. All that reminds him of this event is the scar.

What Is A Scar?

A scar is a place where injury was suffered but also where a healing took place. If you could still feel pain, it would be called a wound. Have you ever looked at a scar and thought about healing? A scar should not only remind you of the injury but it should also remind you of the healing that took place.

Everybody Has Them

We all have physical scars on our bodies. In fact, I'm the one with the scar on the web of my hand between my thumb and index finger. I have scars from the shrapnel of an exploding bullet (it's a long story), multiple biking accidents as a kid, falling off playground equipment, etc.

SCARS OF "LIFE"

Yet what about the scars of "life" that come from those traumatic events of our life from childhood until today? We all have them. The question that I ask here is this: Are they scars or open wounds? It may be healed on the surface, but if something bumps it, does it still send a jolt of pain through your spirit? Yes, I too have had those "injuries of life" that were healed on the surface but when something bumped it, it sent jolts of pain through my spirit. God wants to heal all your wounds of "life" and our text declares it.

INFECTED WOUNDS WILL NEVER HEAL

Yet sometimes we keep the wound infected with sin, unforgiveness, self-pity, doubt or you just keep going back and being re-injured. Sometimes we keep it infected because we believe it would be too painful to really deal with the wound. Yet until we deal with it, it will always stay infected and cause us pain. That wound will ultimately keep you from succeeding and reaching your fullest potential.

SCARS ARE TESTIMONIES

If you have an open wound of "life" go to God and allow Him to pour the "oil and wine" *("oil and wine" are symbols of healing in the Bible)* of His Spirit into your life to bring about healing. I have scars of life and some of them or pretty big scars but they are simply scars. I can point to those scars to testify of God's healing grace. When I see that someone has received an injury such as I did, I can point to my scars to testify to them that God can heal them. I can then testify of how I received my healing and how they can receive theirs.

Scars, no matter how serious the injury that created those scars, remind us of the healing that has taken place.

...He has sent Me to heal the broken-hearted...To console those who mourn in Zion, To give them beauty for ashes, The oil of joy for mourning, The garment of praise for the spirit of heaviness...

Portions from Isa 61:1,3 (NKJV)

THEY HAD BEEN WITH JESUS

ACTS 4:1–13

The tension in the room was so thick you could cut it with a knife. They were faced off with the very people that were responsible for having Jesus crucified and knew they could face the same fate. They were told in no uncertain terms by the High Priest, to stop spreading the news about Jesus or else! Peter stood up and basically told them that they cannot and will not stop telling people about Jesus. We will not stop telling people about who He is, what He has done, what He can do and that He *is* coming back.

A MOST MARVELOUS TESTIMONY

This group of the High Priest's council marveled at the boldness of Peter and the rest of the disciples. Then one of the most complimentary observations was made by this council and it is a compliment that every Christian should have. "*They realized that they had been with Jesus.*"

This council saw something in these disciples that seemed familiar. They saw something in the eyes of these men. They heard something in their speech. They saw something in their disposition. There was just something different about their presence but something that seemed recently familiar. Then they realized that these disciples had been with Jesus and that Jesus had rubbed off on them.

EXTREMELY CONVICTING QUESTION

The extremely convicting question is can people realize that you've been with Jesus? What do people see when they look into your eyes? Do they see what they'd see if they were looking into the eyes of Jesus? What do people hear when they hear you speak? What do they see when they observe your life? Can they realize that you have been with Jesus?

The only way to exude Jesus is spend time with Him. How, by getting into the Word, getting into your prayer closet and all throughout the day talking with Him and asking Him for guidance.

"They realized that they had been with Jesus."

JESUS CAN RELATE

ISA 53; HEB 4:14–16; ROM 8:28; 1 PET 5:6–7

It was a cold and dreary, wind swept, rainy day with a chill that cut to the bone. The drive home from the doctor's office was one of silent sorrow, except for the occasional sob from my wife as she coped with accepting the news the doctor had just relayed. The child that was conceived in her womb was dead. Even though neither one of us had held the child in our hands or looked upon its face, there was still this tide of grief that swelled our hearts as if we had. We know that one day we will see this child in heaven because life begins at conception.

THE PAIN AND SORROW

For the next several weeks in my prayer time, all I could do is weep before God and say "it hurts God, it hurts!" I had to face the struggle that many face in times of grief and that is blaming God for allowing this to happen. The devil is always standing there pointing an accusing finger at God. He did in the Garden of Eden and he's still doing it today.

I wept my way through that struggle and then found myself swimming in this seemingly bottomless ocean of grief. All I could do is tread water.

Going through this I remembered what I had told others in their times of grief: "God understands and He's going to carry you through if you'll hold on to His unchanging hand." I could feel His presence there in my weeping and sorrow. He was there in my pain and grief. He was there in my anger and numbness. He truly was a High Priest that could identify with my struggles.

How Can Jesus Relate?

Some would say, "But how can God feel the pain and anger that we feel when we are tempted to blame Him for allowing 'bad things' to happen?" Well you know God could have pointed an accusing finger at all humanity and said, "You're the reason why My Son is dead!"

When Jesus put on the robe of flesh, He became susceptible to every temptation and pain that all humanity would face. In fact, the prophet Isaiah declared that Jesus would be, "A man of sorrows and acquainted with grief."

He Did It On Purpose

The Son of God purposely came down and took on the robe of flesh to not only feel our pain and grief but to bear them for us! As a child of God, when I go through pain and grief, Christ is there carrying the heaviest part. Too many times, we carry more of the load than we should. Too many times, we fail to come to our High Priest and cast all our cares upon Him.

Saint And Sinner Alike

Yes in this life, whether saint or sinner, you will face pain and sorrow, anguish and toil. However, for the child of God you have One that can acutely identify with your struggles.

You have One that you can take your struggles to and cast your cares upon. You have One that will shoulder the heaviest part for you and walk with you through this time in your life. You have a great refuge called the throne of grace that you can go to, obtain mercy, and find grace to help in your time of need.

Being a child of God does not exempt us from the pain of life. However, it does give us One that will shoulder the load, walk with us, and at times carry us through the pain and sorrow. One thing about being a child of God is that you are going *through* the sorrow and not camping in it. So take it to the LORD in prayer and let Him shoulder the heaviest part.

> "Weeping may endure for a night, But joy comes in the morning."
>
> *Psa* 30:5*b* (NKJV)

SHALL I PURSUE?

1 SAM 30:6–8; JAMES 1:5–8

As a teenager, David was sent by his father to check on his older brothers and see how the battle was going between Israel and the Philistines. As young David approached the front lines, the battle cries of the army of Israel stirred young David's heart with such adrenalin that he ran behind them as they charged to the battlefront. Suddenly, in full stride, every man stopped dead in his tracks and silence filled the air. David was stupefied at what happened next. An uncircumcised Philistine giant stood between them and the Philistine army uttering curses at God Almighty. David was simply incensed at what the giant was saying about God and His ability to help Israel.

YOU JUST KNOW

David didn't need to ask God if he should pursue this giant, he just knew it was the right thing to do. Obviously, it was because God was with him and gave him the victory.

Sometimes in life you don't have to ask God if you need

to pursue because you just know it's the right thing to do. Then there are times when you don't know if or what you should pursue.

YOU'RE HAVING A BAD DAY?

In 1 Sam 30, David was in a grave situation. Put yourself in his shoes. When he was in his late teens the prophet Samuel anointed him to be the King of Israel. For over 13 years, you've been on the run because King Saul is hunting your life like an animal. You're an outcast, a wanted man, a refuge, and a leader of the same. David had several hundred men that were wanted outcast of Israel join him throughout the years. These were men with a price on their heads and the edge of their swords was stained with the blood of men they've killed in battle. You've just come from four days of hard riding on the back of a beast and when you arrive home, your city lies in ashes. All the women and children have been taken as slaves by brutal men. Because of all this, David's band of renegade men was talking of killing him.

YOU MUST HEAR FROM GOD!

In those times of uncertainty you must hear from God. Nevertheless, how do you do that when life is screaming at you and seemingly coming apart at the seams?

Go back and read what David did in 1 Sam 30:6–8. First, he didn't allow the circumstances surrounding him dictate what he was to do. What he did was strengthen himself in the LORD, meaning he focused on what God had done in the past in his life and the life of other great saints of old. Then he sought the presence of God. He shut the world out with all its circumstances and opened himself to God. Then he asked God, "Shall I pursue?"

MY EXAMPLE

In my life when I seek God with "shall I pursue" questions here's what I do:

Steal away with God and seek God's Word to see what it says about my—"shall I pursue." Sometimes the Word doesn't specifically address my "shall I pursue," i.e. a career decision, financial decision, etc. Therefore, I seek to see what principles there are in the Bible that address my "shall I pursue."

Then I ask God for wisdom to understand his Word and will.

If I have multiple choices and I don't have a clear answer, I do the following: In my mind, I'll make my mind up on one answer as if I'm going to pursue that course of action. Then I'll examine my heart for the level of peace I feel. Then I'll back up and make my mind up for the second choice of action I could take. Again, I examine my heart for the level of peace.

Ultimately I'll go with the decision that I have the peace of God in. Sometimes that decision doesn't make much sense in the natural but I have found that when I have peace, "I can pursue," with confidence.

SHALL I PURSUE?

What questions of "shall I pursue" do you face? Remember there are some situations that you don't need to ask you just know it's the right thing to do. But for the rest it's best to console with God before you launch off and pursue because you may pursue what you're not supposed to.

WHAT'S IN YOUR HEART?
JER 17:9–10; 1 TIM 4:1–2; HEB 4:12

Every person's life on that ship was now in grave jeopardy. The ship's hull had been gouged by the rocks under the surface and was taking on water. The area was called "black rock gorge" because the rocks under the surface were black and you couldn't tell how far they reached towards the surface. From the ship's deck it looked as if the rocks were hundreds of feet below the surface. The captain realized too late that it was a deceitful sight he had gazed upon. Now lives were in jeopardy because of his acting upon deception.

> The heart *is* deceitful above all *things,* And desperately wicked; Who can know it?
>
> Jer 17:9 (NKJV)

In the Garden of Eden, the heart of Adam and Eve belonged to God and they knew their hearts completely. However, when Adam and Eve sinned they didn't know their hearts any more. Deceit now had a powerful foothold in the hearts of humanity.

WHAT IS DECEIT?

Deceit is a lie presented as truth. Deception believes a lie is truth. Being deceived is acting upon the lie as being the truth. That's exactly what happened in the Garden of Eden. The devil presented a lie as the truth. Eve believed the lie to be truth and then acted upon the lie as being truth. Therefore, our hearts are prone to believe lies as the truth.

Throughout the years I have watched "Christians" believe a lie as the truth. "I can do this (this being sin) and still be okay with God." "I can participate in this and still be okay with God." The Bible warns us that in the Last Days there will be "doctrines of demons" loosed upon humanity. This is not so much "devil worship" doctrines, as it is lies that steer people away from Christ. Oh, many of these "doctrines" sound religious and some even sound Christian, but anything that doesn't have Christ as the centerpiece is off base.

God asked a question:

> The heart is deceitful above all things, And desperately wicked; Who can know it?
>
> Jer 17:9 (NKJV)

God then gives the answer:

> I, the LORD, search the heart, I test the mind …
>
> Jer 17:10a (NKJV)

The truth is the Word and the Word is Christ. The Holy Spirit will lead you into all truth. So for the Christian our safe harbor from deception is the Word and the Spirit. The Word and the Spirit search our heart to reveal what's really there. (see *Heb* 4:12) Once you know what's there it's up to you to deal with it. However, know this, the longer you fail to deal with it the more likely you'll be deceived into thinking it can stay. The longer it stays the more likely you are to act upon it being the truth.

DO YOU KNOW WHAT'S IN YOUR HEART?

> *I, the* LORD, *search the heart, I test the mind, Even to give every man according to his ways, According to the fruit of his doings.*
>
> *Jer* 19:10 *(*NJKV*)*

Another Gospel

I marvel that you are turning away so soon from Him who called you in the grace of Christ, to a different gospel.

Gal 1:6 (NKJV)

Now the Spirit expressly says that in latter times some will depart from the faith, giving heed to deceiving spirits and doctrines of demons.

1 Tim 4:1 (NKJV)

Having a form of godliness but denying its power. And from such people turn away!

2 Tim 3:5 (NKJV)

The Devil's Tactic

From the inception of the church, the devil and his legion of demons have been trying to derail the church by shifting it from the Gospel of Christ to another gospel. The Greek word for gospel literally means "good news." When you read our various devotional scriptures today, you will see that there is no other gospel. So why are so many "Christians" turning aside to another gospel?

The Devil's Ally

When one comes to Christ, they are a new creation, they've been born again and one can only be born again by accepting the real gospel. One thing that every Christian is to do on a constant basis is crucify and subdue the Adamic nature. The Adamic nature is always seeking ways to fulfill its desires and stray away from God. If that nature is not consistently subdued, it will eventually wreck your faith in the real gospel, either by going back into sin or accepting another gospel.

A New Revelation?

Being a Pentecostal I've seen too many "Pentecostal/Charismatics" stray from the gospel to another gospel. They have these "fresh revelations" from God, but these revelations move the focus from Christ. Anything "revelation" or "doctrine" that moves Christ from the center or foundation is another gospel. It doesn't matter what "spiritual experience" they may have had during this revelation, if it moves Christ from being the center and foundation it's a spurious revelation. The Apostle Paul said that even if an angel from heaven came and proclaimed another gospel, it's a fraud.

Itching Ears

Too many times, I've watched "Christians" willingly accept another gospel because it allowed them to partake of their carnal lustful appetites. Their itching ears of carnality tuned into this other gospel. They have a form of godliness but deny the power thereof. The power of godliness is Christ and His cross, The Gospel.

> Beloved, do not believe every spirit, but test the spirits, whether they are of God...
>
> 1 John 4:1a (NKJV)

Test the teachings you are receiving, including from me, with the acid test of "The Gospel of Christ." Any teaching, doctrine, revelation, etc., which moves Christ from the center and foundation is a dangerous "other gospel."

What "gospel" are you adhering to? Are you accepting teachings that appeal to your carnal appetites? Are you simply accepting doctrines based upon the presenters "charisma" or "revelation" they had? Are you testing and trying the spirits? God will never say or reveal anything that's not already in His Word.

What "gospel" are you going after?

GOD GIVE ME CROP FAILURE
GEN 8:22; GAL 6:7–9; 2 COR 12:8–10

A FALLEN WORLD

Have you ever noticed that you don't have to plant weed seed. Ever notice that you don't have to water or fertilize weeds to get them to grow? Ever notice that grass grows better through the cracks of your driveway than in your yard? All of these are a result of a fallen world.

SEEDTIME AND HARVEST

There are laws that God has established. One is seedtime and harvest. That's not only for physical seed but spiritual as well. Our Gal 6 text proclaims this law of seedtime and harvest. Many times I have seen people commit sins and then come to God to "get right," but they wanted crop failure for all the carnal seeds of sin they had sown. I have also seen most of them fall away from God when crop failure doesn't come.

"YOU REAP WHAT YOU SOW!"

It's a law, which unless God does a miracle, will be enforced. King David had found forgiveness and grace from God for the sin of adultery and murder, yet there was a physical price to pay for those sins. There was the death of the innocent baby that was a product of his adulterous affair. There was the price of strife within his household, "the sword will never depart from your house." It would also appear to me that David's kingdom was never as strong as it was before his sins adultery and murder.

DOES GOD EVER INTERVENE?

Yes! He intervened in David's life. According to the Mosaic Law, David was to have been led outside the city gates and the elders of Israel were to execute him by stoning. God intervened! I have also have known of individuals who were humbly repentant and willing to take responsibility for their actions, which would include jail, and prison time but God miraculously intervened.

BOTTOM LINE IS THIS.

If you have sown carnal seeds you are going to get a carnal harvest so what to do? First, truly repent from your heart and turn away from sinning. Secondly, accept the consequences of your actions and the harvest that comes from those actions. Thirdly and more importantly, begin to sow the good seeds of God's Word.

SOWING THE WORD

How do you sow the seed of God's Word? First you have to start reading intently (studying) the Bible. Secondly, love God from your heart and in doing so you will start obeying the Word. Thirdly thank God everyday that your name is written in the Lamb's Book of Life and that you have eternal life. Thank God, for any good you see in your life or around you.

The sooner you get the good seed in the ground, the sooner you're going to have a good harvest. The sooner you stop sowing carnal seeds, the sooner that crop will be over. God's grace will carry you through the ill harvest if you'll trust and follow Him.

> And let us not grow weary while doing good, for in due season we shall reap if we do not lose heart.
>
> Gal 6:9 (NKJV)

Fluffy Biscuits

Rom 5:3–5; James 1:2–4; Deut 8:1–5;
Rom 8:28–30

Cathead Biscuits

If you're from the South, you've probably heard the phrase
"cathead biscuits." That doesn't mean biscuits made from a
cat head, but rather a descriptive term of how big they are.
My grandmother used to make cathead biscuits. I remember as a kid she'd let me help (actually, endure me being in
the way) make cat head biscuits.

The first thing she would do is get a large mixing bowl
and this funny looking silver can. This can was the size of
a coffee can with a handle on the side and a hand crank.
Inside the can, the bottom was open with a metal screen.
There was a metal rod connected to the hand crank that
lightly rubbed against the screen when you turned the crank.
That funny looking can was called a sifter.

Sifted Again

One day as grandma was sifting the flour through the sifter, I asked her why she was doing that. She replied, "to get all the lumps out of the flour." Then after she sifted it once, she would get a second large mixing bowl and sift the flour she had just sifted. I asked her why she was sifting it again and she replied "the more you sift it the fluffier the biscuits." She would sift that same batch of flour three or four times before she'd add the other ingredients. But she did have some of the fluffiest cathead biscuits I'd ever seen.

God's Sifter

You know God has you in a sifter called "life." He's sifting you to get all the lumps and impurities out. You go through one trial and now you're faced with another one. God's sifting you again. Some of you may be saying, "I must be pretty lumpy because God keeps putting me through the sifter!" No doubt, there's truth to that statement but I ask you this, do you keep putting things back into your life that God keeps sifting out? Remember also that the Holy Spirit is in the process of conforming you into the image of Christ and therefore another reason for the sifting. God never does anything to bring you ultimate harm but rather ultimate good. God has the end results of your life in mind, fluffy biscuits.

> And we know that all things work together for good to those who love God, to those who are the called according to His purpose.
>
> Rom 8:28 (NKJV)

From the Obscurity of the Sheep Fields to the Comfort of the Palace

1 Sam 16; 2 Sam 11

The Obscurity of the Sheep Fields

The story of David is a wonderful "rags to riches" story. The youngest of several brothers, always getting the jobs that none of the other brothers wanted to do. It seemed as if David's life would be like most of the youngest siblings of his day, a life of scraps and little inheritance when his father passed away. By the time his other brothers took what they wanted of the inheritance, there wasn't going to be much of anything left for him. He would be poor and His kids would be poor.

One day, David got a call to come in the house. David knew that there was some type of big meeting in the house but also knew he hadn't been invited. When he walked into the room his father and all his brother's were there with an elderly man in the middle. The old man stood up, walked over to David, pours a flask full of oil over David's head, and pronounces David as King of Israel! David was about seventeen years old when this took place. Wow, it appeared that in just a few months he would ascend to the throne of Israel. If you read the story of David's life it was thirteen years of struggle, heartache, pain, and toil before he finally became king of Israel.

THE COMFORT OF THE PALACE

Throughout all the years of toil and struggle, David trusted in God even in the face of insurmountable odds and the constant threat of death. Of course, God always came through for him.

When he became King, God gave David victory over all his enemies of surrounding nations. God gave him all the houses of his former enemy King Saul. God gave him riches, favor, success, and fame. God had brought him from the obscurity of the sheep fields to the comfort of the King's Palace.

WHAT SHEEP FIELDS HAS GOD BROUGHT YOU FROM?

Perhaps there are similarities in your life's story. As you reflect back upon life, you see how you toiled and struggled. You remember the obscurity of the sheep fields. You remember the intense battles of life and how you trusted in God to bring you through and He did. Now compared to then, your life is much easier. You have climbed the ladder so to speak, and now you have more money than ever before. You have status that you didn't have back then. You are in the circle of influential people. You are counted a "success" by those around you.

BORED WITH LIFE

All of these characteristics are seen in King David's life when we come to 2 Sam 11. David became "bored" with life and was blinded by all the "success." He had forgotten where God had brought him from, the sheep fields of obscurity. He had forgotten that it was God and God alone that brought him out of the obscurity of the sheep fields to the comfort of the Palace. Perhaps if he had kept in mind the obscurity of the sheep fields, we wouldn't the tragic events of the adulterous affair and the murder to cover it up.

WHAT ABOUT YOU?

Stop and take an inventory of your life and where you are in "society's" success status. Are you getting board and beginning to explore other venues of life. Do you want to travel in circles of fellowship that really are not spiritually healthy? Are you beginning to justify compromises to your faith? Have you forgotten the obscurity of the sheep fields? These are all things that King David did and thus we have the tragic events and all the fallout that followed starting in 2 Sam 11.

Tragedy awaits you too if you fail to remember where God has brought you from and keep a heart of humble gratefulness.

YOUR SHEEP FIELD

Perhaps you feel that you are currently in the sheep fields of obscurity. If you continue to follow and trust God, one day, He will bring you out of the sheep fields of obscurity. I urge you to make it a point that you will not forget where God has brought you from. Do something that will keep you in remembrance of God's goodness, which has brought you out of the sheep fields and into the palace.

You Can Be A Success!

Proverbs 3:1–10; Deuteronomy 28; 1 Sam 15:20–23

"If you will send me a $100 God will give you a $1,000," the televangelist says with emotional fervor. I've often wondered if the televangelist truly believed it, why doesn't he send me the $100 so God can give him the $1,000? It's just a thought.

I've seen one side of the gamut to the other on prosperity and success. On one side, a Christian is to be a poor heel of society. The other side a Christian should be at the top of every social and material status. However, what does God really desire for His children? He desires for His children to be successful.

The question is what is God's definition of success?

Our society for the most the part measures success based upon status of materials, education, social acceptance, etc. God bases success upon obedience to Him. Obedience to

Him may or may not lead to material gain, educational gain, or acceptance in society, but it will make you successful.

THREE KEYS TO BEING SUCCESSFUL

Over the next three devotionals I am going give you, what I see are three keys to being a success in every area of your life. If you will possess all three of these keys, you will be a success in God's eyes and have a successful future.

THE KEYS ARE NO GOOD UNLESS...

There are so many verses of scripture in the Bible about God's desire for His children to succeed. Although the three keys that I am going to show you over the next few days are a must, those keys will do you no good unless you possess obedience to Him. You cannot claim the blessings of God without first obeying God.

FALSE CLAIMS OF SUCCESS

Many people claim that their success has come from God, but they do not obey Him. Obedience to God must be complete obedience and not partial. King Saul found out in 1 Samuel 15 that in God's eyes, partial obedience is the same as disobedience. Jesus said, "*Seek first the Kingdom of God and His righteousness and all these other things will be added to you*," (Matt 6:33–NKJV).

PRACTICAL APPLICATION

Mark it down, God wants you to succeed! He wants you to succeed in your career; He wants you to succeed in your relationships; He wants you to succeed in your health; He wants you succeed in your ministry. God wants you to succeed! If you want, the three keys to unlock God's success for your life, you are going to have to completely obey God in all areas of your life.

CHALLENGE

Are you obeying God in all areas of your life? Are you seeking success first or God's Kingdom? Do you believe that God truly wants you to succeed? Ask God to show you what areas you need to surrender to Him.

1ST KEY TO SUCCESS—
A PASSION FOR GOD

DEUT 6:4–5; MARK 12:30; PHIL 3:1–14;
JOHN 7:37–39

THERE THEY ARE!

There they are; four fearless guys, bare-chested with war
paint from their face down to their waist. War cries full of
emotion flow from the depths of their soul through their
lips with chilling effect. Their eyes are ablaze with the fire
of passion for victory. They cannot sit still, they are on their
feet pounding their chest and the ground around them.
They mean business and their presence is to strike fear in
the hearts of their opponents. They are consumed by passion. I am not talking about Indian warriors; I'm talking
about those guys you see on TV at the football games! Some
would call those guys radical. Some would call them diehard
fans. Whatever you call them, one thing seems for sure, they
have passion.

Is Passion For God Radical?

Interesting enough, when it comes to the things of God, it would seem by most accounts, that if you truly have a passion for God you take a risk of being labeled a radical. Was the Apostle Paul radical? Was King David radical? Was Daniel radical? Were Shadrach, Meshach, and Abed-Nego radical? Whatever you call them, one thing is for sure, they had a passion for God!

A Passion For God Is The Fuel For All Abundant Life.

This is what gets you out of bed in the morning. It's what separates you from the mundane. It's what sharpens your outlook on life. However, how does one obtain a passion for God and what fuels a continuation of such passion? Just as having a passion for anything in life, it is an act of your will and limited only by your will and faith. Okay, but what separates passion from desire. To me passion is backed with power and actions whereas desire is wanting but lacks power of pursuit.

How Do You Get This Passion With Power?

This type of passion comes from spending time with God *(prayer and communing)* and His Word. It comes from the depth of your love and devotion to God. Jesus said in John 7:37ff that it would be the free flowing river of the Holy Spirit.

Passion Can Wane Even For A Spirit-Filled Believer.

Timothy was a young Spirit-filled preacher that was facing some tough times in ministry. His mentor, the Apostle Paul, could see Timothy's passion waning, so Paul challenged Timothy to fan the flame. *(2 Tim 1:3–7)* From this exhortation of Paul to Timothy, we see that it is a choice of our will.

PRACTICAL APPLICATION

The first key to being a success is a passion for God. Sometimes our passion for God can be snuffed out because we've stacked stuff in our life that doesn't burn on God's altar. We fill our lives with temporal things and our passions become misplaced and misguided. With our lips we state that we want to live a life fueled with Godly passion, but our actions do not support such a testimony. God doesn't mind if we have desires for hobbies and such, so long as they are second to our passion for Him.

CHALLENGE

Today's challenge is to reflect and ask God to show you what you've stacked on His altar of your life that doesn't burn. If you need to repent, repent and clean the altar off and begin to stack God's fuel upon it. *(You do this by spending time communing with God and spending time in His Word.)* Ask God for a fresh fire of the Holy Spirit to set ablaze His fuel you've placed upon His altar in your life. Perhaps you do have passion for God (great!), don't let it wane, but keep pouring on the fuel of the Spirit, the Word and faith.

2ND KEY TO SUCCESS–
A TEACHABLE SPIRIT

PHIL 3:12–14; PSA 95:7–11; I PET 5:5–7

The master potter plopped a lump of clay on the middle of his potter's wheel, splashed a bit of water on the shapeless lump of clay and began to spin the wheel. With his hands in the clay, he began to work his mastery into that lump to create his masterpiece. Every few moments he would splash a bit of water on his work in progress. "Why are you adding water to the clay," asked a young apprentice.

"To keep the clay pliable in my hands," replied the master potter.

"You can never make a masterpiece, unless you keep the clay pliable until you are done and ready to place it in the kiln oven."

KNOW IT ALL

Don't believe it, just ask them. They have this attitude of, "been there, done that, know all about it, so I don't need to hear it any more." It may be true in some things, but they carry this attitude in all areas of their life. They are not open to receive instruction and thus are not open to receive correction.

YOU'RE NOT STUPID ARE YOU?

One of my favorite verses of the Bible in regards to teaching my kids is Proverbs 12:1, but this verse is for all ages. "Whoever loves instruction loves knowledge, but he who hates correction *is* stupid," (NKJV). One who hates correction is one that does not possess a teachable spirit. You're not stupid are you?

THE APOSTLE PAUL KNEW MORE THAN US BUT HE WASN'T STUPID!

The Apostle Paul received revelations of God in such depths that God would not allow him to share them with anyone. Paul, a man that God used in mighty miracles and in such ways that even a sweat cloth taken from his body had power to heal people. Paul, a man that demons trembled to see coming, a man that God used plant hundreds of churches and mentor dozens of ministers. Paul, a man that God used to pen two thirds of the New Testament, was a man that possessed a teachable spirit from the day of his conversion to the day he died. We know this because of what he said in Phil 3:12–14. Paul wrote this about four years before his death.

CALL IT WHAT IT IS, PRIDE!

When you cease to have a teachable spirit, you become puffed up and arrogant. You begin to harden your heart and become deceived into thinking that you have greater knowledge than others and no one really has anything to offer you that you don't already know. Oh, you may not say that out loud, but it is portrayed in your attitude. That's called "pride" and it will be your downfall.

Look at these verses along with the text verses I have given.

For if anyone thinks himself to be something,
when he is nothing, he deceives himself.

Gal 6:3 (NKJV)

A man's pride will bring him low, But the
humble in spirit will retain honor.

Prov 29:23 (NKJV)

For thus says the High and Lofty One who
inhabits eternity, whose name *is* Holy: "I dwell
in the high and holy *place*, With him *who* has a
contrite and humble spirit, To revive the spirit
of the humble, And to revive the heart of the
contrite ones.

Isa 57:15 (NKJV)

He who disdains instruction despises his own
soul, But he who heeds rebuke gets understanding.

Prov 15:32 (NKJV)

PRACTICAL APPLICATION

You may have all the talent in the world but if you do not
have a teachable spirit, you are of no use to God and His
kingdom. Do you have a teachable spirit? Here's a test that
might help you discern if you do or not.

If you are being corrected and the correction is right, do
you bristle up at the one correcting you?

Do you find yourself more than not telling people how
"it" should be done?

If you read a book by a noted author, do you say at the

end of the book, "I knew all that anyway, so the book was boring to me?"

Do you think, "I don't need anyone to tell me how to do it?"

Did you get this far in the questions?

ANSWER KEY

For one that does not have a teachable spirit, he/she would answer the questions as follows:

1–yes, 2–yes, 3–yes, 4–yes, 5–no.

If you answered 3 or more as answered above, then you probably do not have as flexible and teachable spirit as you might think. You need to let God deal with you about this.

CHALLENGE

Are you letting God splash water on you, or are you putting up an umbrella? Ask God to show you if you have a teachable spirit or not.

3ʳᵈ Key To Be A Success–
A Good Work Ethic

Luke 17:5–10; Eph 6:5–8; Col 3:22–25; 1 Tim 6:1–2; Titus 2:9–10

"I'm *not* doing any more until I get paid more," grumbled the worker. "If the boss wants more then he's going have to come to the table with a better offer." Have you ever heard someone say this? I have and I can tell you that they will never be paid enough. They have the attitude of doing the least amount of work for the greatest amount of return.

I'm Entitled To It!

Yes, I do understand that there are companies that take advantage of their workers and that perhaps one of the original ambitions of unions was to step in and help the workers not be taken advantage of. Yet today there's an overriding mentality that wants more for less. It's almost a mentality of entitlement. There used to be a saying, "honest days work for an honest days pay," but that's rarely the case it seems today.

MY PERSONAL EXPERIENCE

When I was in college, I worked for *UPS*. I was a part-time driver working 15–20 hours a week. I got two weeks paid vacation, a personal holiday, several other paid holidays, an option week that I could take off with pay, or get an extra week of pay. I had full medical benefits with dental and vision riders. My starting pay was around $10 and hour and in three years I was making over $13 an hour and this was back in mid 90's. Yes, it was a union job and I know because it was a union job I had all those benefits. The mafia, I mean the union, did a great job. Yet, there was an attitude among many of the workers that it wasn't enough and they were not going to give more until they got more. Okay, at that time, in that part of the country, the average full-time driver was making 20+ an hour!

WHAT DID JESUS SAY A GOOD WORK ETHIC IS?

Jesus gives a parable that tells us that our faith is going to be lived out through a good work ethic. What is a good work ethic? Well according to Jesus' parable in Luke 16 a good work ethic is not doing what's required of you. A good work ethic is doing more than what's required of you. It's going the extra mile without having being asked to do so.

PRACTICAL APPLICATION

What kind of work ethic do you have? You will see time and time again in our scripture, texts that a good work ethic is required to be a success.

On the same hand, you don't have to let the employer take unfair advantage of you. But even in that setting, you still have to have a good work ethic.

When you go to work, do you understand that you are really working for God? Even if you are self-employed, your work is a reflection of your faith in God because He's the One that you are really working for.

CHALLENGE

So is your attitude "I'm not going to give more until I get more?" If it is, you need to spend some time with God asking Him to forgive you and for Him to show why you feel that way. I must confess in times past, I too have been caught up in society's *entitlement* mentality and I've had to repent.

It may be that you are being taken advantage of by your employer. If so, ask God to show you what to do. However, if it's because you've bought into society's *entitlement* mentality you need to repent.

THE HAUNTED HOUSE!

HEB 12:1–2; MATT 23:27–28; JER 17:9–10;
PSA 19:12–14; NUM 32:23; MARK 4:22–23

Do you live in a haunted house? What ... you don't believe
in ghosts? You don't have any dark, shadowy rooms in your
house that you keep the door closed to all the times? You
fear what's behind that door because you hear the rattling of
skeletons bones and the moans of tortured souls. Just to walk
past it gives you the heebee geebeeies! When your friends or
company come calling, you keep them away from that room
because you don't want anyone to know about it.

THE REAL HAUNTED HOUSE

Well the house I am talking about is not your physical
dwelling but rather your heart. You may be haunted by your
past or past sins, *(I have dealt with that in my devotional "I
Wish I Hadn't Done That")*.

You may be haunted by secret sins you hide in that room.
Those secret sins scratch and claw to get out. Instead of letting them out, you slip behind the door to entertain them,

thinking that that might appease them. But alas, no sooner have you slipped out of the room and shut the door that they start scratching and clawing once again. Am I getting close to the door of your haunted room?

DO YOU REALLY BELIEVE GOD SEES IT ALL?

Well we all have *cognitive* knowledge that God sees every room in our heart and that nothing is hidden from Him. But dare I say our heart knowledge of that isn't in full belief! If your heart truly believed that, you would not be doing those "secret" things that you don't want anyone to know about. Dare I say that if we all believed that, our lives would be lived much, much differently?

DID KING DAVID BELIEVE THAT GOD SEES IT ALL?

When David conceived in his heart to commit adultery with Bathsheba he knew it was wrong but he did it any way because he thought he could keep it a secret. However, she came up pregnant. *Ooops!* So to cover it up he called her husband home from the battlefield thinking that he was an ordinary man and would (well you know), but he didn't. When that plan to cover up his "secret sin" didn't work, you know what David did next; he essentially had the man murdered. David thought that it was a secret and that everything would stay hidden. But when God confronted David God said:

> For you did *it* secretly, but I will do this thing before all Israel, before the sun.
>
> 2 Sam 12:12 (NKJV)

God gives us all room to repent but when we come to the end of that room God will confront us and He will expose us. You know one of the reasons why God exposes us is because He loves us. It's much better if we repent and confess our sins rather than have Him expose us.

PRACTICAL APPLICATION

To be truthful, you and I both have had or have some secret rooms in our hearts. Rooms that house our thoughts that we hope are never spoken aloud, our little sins, our compromises, our dark side; our dirty laundry so to speak. You hear the skeletons shaking in the closet.

I AM AFRAID OF WHAT'S BEHIND THAT DOOR!

It started out as a little sin but now has grown into a horrible monster. It has grown into something that is so terrifying you are consumed with a paralyzing fear at the thought of confronting such a hideous beast. It is pounding on the door threatening to wreak havoc in your life. You know that if that beast breaks down the door and gets out, it will completely ruin your life and perhaps the lives of others. You feel trapped so what do you do?

CHALLENGE

First, don't believe that you can allow that "little sin" to live in your life. Sin never stays "little"!

This is not an easy challenge.

Repent and ask Jesus to forgive you and to clean out the "secret" rooms in your life. Pray what King David prayed and had learned in the latter years of his life:

> Search me, O God, and know my heart; Try me, and know my anxieties; 24And see if *there is any* wicked way in me, And lead me in the way everlasting.
>
> Psa 139:23–24 (NKJV)

That was the easy part this next part gets a bit tricky but is necessary if your "little secret sin" becomes a perpetual cycle.

> Confess *your* trespasses to one another, and pray
> for one another, that you may be healed...
>
> James 5:16a (NKJV)

You need a trusted Christian, which could be your spouse, a friend, anyone that you can really trust. Tell them of the struggle you are having and that you need them to help you.

First thing they can do to help you is not tell others about this struggle.

The second thing they can do is promise you that they will ask you the tough questions to help keep that "little sin" from creeping back into your life.

The third thing they can do is pray for you and with you.

IT'S JUST ORANGES

JOHN 4:35–38; MATT 9:35–38

It was a comfortable warm spring morning, and the air was saturated with the smell of sweet orange blossoms. Polk County Florida used to, and still may, boast of being the orange growing capital of the world. When I lived in Polk County for a few years, I experienced the wonderful fragrance of orange blossoms that words cannot accurately describe. The closest I can come to describing it is the smell of orange muffins baking in the oven.

There were orange groves everywhere, and I mean everywhere. There were hundreds of thousands of orange trees, and in full season there could easily be millions of oranges. Being new to the area, it was quite intriguing watching the progress of the trees going from blossom to small green oranges to fully ripened and ready for harvesting. Once the oranges reached their ripened perfection, I noticed something extremely odd; really, it was quite baffling.

WHAT'S GOING ON HERE?

Although many of the groves were bustling with harvesters, many of the groves remained untouched. I thought, surely someone would come along and harvest all these oranges. Day by day, I watched as more of the luscious fruit fell from the tree to the ground. Day by day, I watched what once were ripened oranges slowly rot and decay. I couldn't stand it any longer, so I asked a local why they let so many oranges go to waste. He looked at me like I had two heads and responded, "It's just oranges." They had become so used to the cycle of the fruit that they didn't give all the untouched oranges a second look.

THERE ARE ORANGES ALL AROUND US

You know, there are many ripened oranges around us; they are called souls. Dare I say we've become so used to them being lost that we don't give their soul a second look. There are two very sad verses in the Bible, yet these two verses peer into the plight and lostness of humanity.

> Look on *my* right hand and see, For *there is* no one who acknowledges me; Refuge has failed me; No one cares for my soul.
>
> Psa 142:4 (NKJV)

> That at that time you were without Christ, being aliens from the commonwealth of Israel and strangers from the covenants of promise, having no hope and without God in the world.
>
> Eph 2:12 (NKJV)

PRACTICAL APPLICATION

As you go throughout the day and come in contact with those that you know are lost and without Jesus, remember, they're all oranges. Ask Jesus to let you see what He sees in those *"oranges."* Ask Jesus to let you feel what He feels for those *"oranges."* Ask Jesus to use you to pick some *"oranges."*

WHAT WILL BE SAID IN YOUR EULOGY

PROV 22:1

DEARLY BELOVED, WE ARE GATHERED
HERE TODAY TO PAY OUR FINAL RESPECTS...

Have you ever wondered what will be said about you at your funeral? I know it sounds morbid to even ponder such thoughts, but think about it. It's all said and done in this life, and now people are gathered together to think about you and your life. Did you live a good life? Did you achieve "success" in this life? Were you a good person? What will they remember most about you? What will they say about you at your funeral?

I heard a story of a man who wanted to know who would attend his funeral and what would be said about him at his funeral. To do this, he faked his death with only the funeral director in on his scheme. The casket was closed, but he was hidden out of sight to observe who was there and what was said. I imagine that when his family and friends discovered he wasn't dead they would probably take care of that.

DON'T MAKE IT HARD FOR THE PREACHER

Don't make it hard for the preacher say something wonderful about you! As a pastor, I've done more funerals than I'd like to remember. I don't think that a funeral can ever be easy, but some people make it easier by how they lived their life. Others make it plain ole hard for me, because I cannot lie yet must be sensitive about the moment at hand.

> A *good* name is to be chosen rather than great riches, Loving favor rather than silver and gold.
>
> Prov 22:1 (NKJV)

PRACTICAL APPLICATION

A friend of mine has a saying that is attached to all her emails:
"Life is a coin. You can spend it anyway you wish, but you can only spend it once."

How are you spending your life? What are you doing to build and keep a good name? It's never too late to start building that good name. It's never too late to start giving the preacher some good things to say about you at your funeral.

Most importantly, what you want to hear when you pass from this life into eternity is the LORD say, "Well done my good and faithful servant." If you've lived your life to hear the LORD say that, then they'll have good things to say about you at your funeral.

CHALLENGE

Ask yourself the question, "What will they say about me at my funeral?" Ask the LORD to show you how to build a good name above all the riches and accolades the world has to offer. Strive to live your life to hear the LORD say, "Well done my good and faithful servant."

FROM THE MASTER'S HAND

PSA 121:1–8; PHIL 4:19; MATT 7:7–11

PAVLOV'S DOGS?

The sound that a chip bag makes when being opened is a familiar sound, especially to the dogs in our house. They know just about every sound associated with food, and when they hear it, they come running.

Throughout the years, I have had several shelties, and I would teach them to do tricks. One of which was teaching them to catch the treats I would throw their way. There was about a ten month period when I was building a house, and as a result, my family and I had to live with my mom, who had an inside dog. Whenever I was eating something, both chowhounds were there.

LOOKING AT THE RESULTS OR THE SOURCE OF THE RESULTS?

One day I noticed something different about the two dogs. When I had food, my dog was watching every move my hand was making while my mom's dog was scanning the floor for any crumbs that may fall. Both dogs had anticipation, but one was watching the floor while the other was watching the master's hand.

> Unto You I lift up my eyes, O You who dwell in the heavens. ² Behold, as the eyes of servants look to the hand of their masters, As the eyes of a maid to the hand of her mistress, So our eyes look to the Lord our God, Until He has mercy on us.
>
> Psa 123:1–2 (NKJV)

PRACTICAL APPLICATION AND CHALLENGE

I propose two questions to you. Are you watching the floor of life hoping to find any crumbs of blessings, or are you watching the master's hand for the blessings and provisions of life? By the way, many times I would pull my hand up towards my face and my dog would follow my hand, and then I could make eye contact with him and talk to him.

Every good and perfect gift comes from the Father of lights with whom there is no shadow of turning.

I Don't Smell Anything!

Matt 7:1–5

"Man you stink!"

That's a common phrase I get from my wife when I come in from mowing the yard in the summer. "I don't smell anything," is my common response. It's true; I really don't smell anything. It's not that my sense of smell is bad, quite the opposite. My wife says I smell like a dog. No, that didn't come out right; I have a nose like a dog. No, that didn't come out right either. My sense of smell is like that of a dog. Okay, that's right.

So why can't I smell anything?

It's because when I'm working in the yard, my stench slowly increases, and thus my nose becomes used to the smell as it rises. So, I really cannot tell how bad I stink. Now if you can smell yourself, then you sure enough stink!

You know many people can't smell themselves. I'm not talking about their body odor, but their attitude odor. They talk about other's attitudes and cannot smell their own. People around them can smell their attitude, and man, it stinks. They cannot smell themselves, because they've become so used to their smelly attitude. Sometimes we need a friend to tell us we stink.

PRACTICAL APPLICATION

What to do? Take a bath! Take a bath in God's presence. Take a bath in God's Word. Take a bath in God's river—the Holy Spirit. Put on some deodorant of the fruit of the Spirit, and let the fragrance of Christ abound.

CHALLENGE

So how do you smell? Why not ask your spouse or a close friend.

AT THE END OF THE DAY

What matters at the end of the day? When you've cut out all the lights and you are laying there in bed thinking about the day's events; what really matters? The tasks that you didn't complete? The people you didn't make contact with? The opinion of others about you?

PUT ME AT THE TOP OF YOUR LIST!!!

We strive for so much in today's society. There are so many things that clamor for us to put them at the top of our list of "what matters." Have you noticed though that the list of "what matters" is constantly changing? Someone has convinced you to put their priority at the top of your "what matters" list.

Being a pastor, you'd think I would have known what matters, but I didn't, and I have discovered that many pastors really don't know either. It's not about job performance, pleasing others, etc...What really matters isn't your job performance, your bank account, civic events, kid's events, family events, what others think about you...

Revolution!

If all Christians would solidify what really matters, I cannot begin to imagine the impact Christians would truly have in this world. If you solidify this in your life, it will go along way in helping reduce the stress of what to put at the top of your daily "to do list." If you'll put this at the top of your "what matters" list and stick to accomplishing just this one thing it will revolutionize you life.

I don't mean to put it at the top of the list out of a sense of "Christian duty." It must be there because you truly know and believe that that's where it should be. You must put this at the top of your "what matters" list and then only put things on your list that will be in agreement with fulfilling it throughout your day. If you put this at the top of your "what matters" list, it will help you in your relationships, your job, your finances, everything in life!

Token List

Oh, there are quite a few Christians who "say" they have this at the top of their list. One must question how hard they are working at accomplishing it, because their priorities and fruit in life do not reflect that this truly is atop of their "what matters" list.

When you lay down at night the one question that you must ask yourself is, "Did I do what really matters?" So, what is it that must be at the top of every Christian's "what matters" list? Obedience.

Please read the following: Deut 10:12; Deut 11:13; Deut 26:16

Partial Obedience is Equal to Disobedience

Please read 1 Sam 15:1–31 to better understand the rest of this devotional. King Saul was told by God what to do, but Saul only partially obeyed God. However, we see that in God's eyes partial obedience to Him is the same as disobedience. I tell you this is something I have seen many Christians do at some time or another, including myself. Look at what God said to King Saul about his justified partial obedience.

> So Samuel said: "Has the LORD *as great* delight in burnt offerings and sacrifices, As in obeying the voice of the LORD? Behold, to obey is better than sacrifice, And to heed than the fat of rams.
>
> 1 Sam 15:22 (NKJV)

THE ONE QUESTION

So when you are laying down tonight, you must answer the question which really matters, and that is "Have I obeyed God?" If the answer is yes, then that's all that matters. If the answer is no, then ask God to forgive you, and tomorrow start fresh by putting what really matters at the top of your list.

WHAT ARE YOU THINKING?

PHIL 4:4–8; PSA 19:14; MARK 7:20–23; MATT 12:34–37; 2 COR 10:3–6

What were you thinking about before you started reading this devotional? Have you ever thought about how many thoughts go through your cognitive mind every day, every week, every month, every year, since you were born? Our mind has had billions upon billions of thought processes and yet what are we really thinking about? How vain are most of our thoughts? How selfish are most of our thoughts? How deceived are our thoughts?

HOW POWERFUL ARE OUR THOUGHTS?

Without getting too theological on the dichotomy of our person, let me say that the Bible says that out of our heart comes our thoughts, which guide our speech and behavior. Ever heard, "out of the abundance of the heart the mouth speaks?" When you read our text in Mark and Mathew, you will see that sin starts in our thoughts. Proverbs says "as one thinks in his heart so is he."

Thoughts guide us in our actions, the way we feel, the way we see life, the way we treat others and what we say. Thoughts are so powerful that the Bible says that we are to "renew our minds" (Rom 12:1–2, NKJV) in the Word.

PRACTICAL APPLICATION

If your faith is weak then I ask you to question what you are thinking. If you are angry, what are you thinking? If you are lusting then what are you thinking? If you harbor un-for-giveness then what are you thinking? If you are struggling with temptations then what are you thinking? If you are struggling with your thoughts then what are you thinking? If you have a bad attitude then what you thinking?

CHALLENGE

Our text in Phil 4 shows us how to overcome those struggles we struggle with. Also, 2 Cor 10 shows us how to bring our thoughts into spiritual subjection. What are you thinking?

WORSHIP LIKE A DEER

Psa 42:1–2; Psa 63:1; John 4:13–14

When a deer pants for the water, it could be that he has just come from fleeing an enemy trying to kill him. He is now thirsty and puts all his senses into finding water. He feels the ground because the ground has a certain feel the closer you get to water. He uses his sense of smell because there are certain smells around water. He uses his sense of sight because there is certain vegetation that grows near water. He uses his sense of hearing because other animals make certain sounds when they are near water.

> As the deer pants for the water brooks, So pants my soul for You, O God.
>
> Psa 42:1 (NKJV)

LIFE

This life is draining to say the least. Spiritually the world is a dry and barren land. Our spirit man becomes dry and thirsty. Therefore, the antidote is to worship like a deer.

I imagine that as King David was meditating on his intense need and desire for God's presence an image from his youthful days as a shepherd raced across his mind. He remembered watching a deer search for water and that image capsulated his emotions perfectly. For David nothing else mattered; it was a life or death situation to him. He was either going to find God's presence or he would die.

WHAT IS YOUR SOURCE?

How about you? How intense are you in worshipping God? Are you seeking God's presence to satisfy your thirsty soul or are you drinking from what the world is offering? Are you drinking from the world's "self-help" fountain? Are you drinking from the world's "escape" fountain of alcohol and drugs? Yes, there are those who are "Christians" that use alcohol and drugs to "cope" with life and think that it is somehow going to satisfy their thirsty soul. Are you drinking from the world's fountain of "success" and "material gain"?

> Jesus answered and said to her, "Whoever drinks of this water will thirst again, 14but whoever drinks of the water that I shall give him will never thirst. But the water that I shall give him will become in him a fountain of water springing up into everlasting life."
>
> John 4:13–14 (NKJV)

NOTHING ELSE

There is nothing that is going to satisfy your thirsty spirit except God's presence, His Word and His Spirit. Seek God with everything you have, put all yourself into seeking Him. Sometimes you may try, but you're not putting your all into seeking Him. You have to put your all into seeking God to find Him.

And you will seek Me and find Me, when you
search for Me with all your heart.

Jer 29:13 (NKJV)

I encourage you to read the following passages: Psa 9:1;
Psa 111:1; Psa 119:2,11,34,58,145; Psa 138:1. Worship like a deer
and you will find God's satisfying presence.

THE SEED AND THE SOIL

MARK 4:1–20

"Listen! Behold, a sower went out to sow. ⁴And it happened, as he sowed, *that* some *seed* fell by the wayside; and the birds of the air came and devoured it. ⁵Some fell on stony ground, where it did not have much earth; and immediately it sprang up because it had no depth of earth. ⁶But when the sun was up it was scorched, and because it had no root it withered away. ⁷And some *seed* fell among thorns; and the thorns grew up and choked it, and it yielded no crop. ⁸But other *seed* fell on good ground and yielded a crop that sprang up, increased and produced: some thirtyfold, some sixty and some a hundred." ⁹And He said to them, "He who has ears to hear, let him hear!"

Mark 4:3–9 (NKJV)

Bringing God's Word Down To Earth

God said that His ways are higher than our ways and His thoughts higher than ours. Therefore, when Jesus, God in flesh, walked this earth He would use common everyday items or events to draw upon analogies of the Kingdom of God. One analogy that He used quite frequently was agriculture, because the society at that time was mainly agricultural. Although Jesus spoke this parable almost 2,000 years ago, its application is fresh for you today.

This Is What It Says

The bottom line of this parable is this: The seed is the Word of God and the soil is your heart and life. The point is this: Which soil are you? No really, which one; not which one you *think* you are, but which one is really your heart? How can you tell?

The Challenge

Over the next few devotionals, we are going to take a fresh look at this parable and apply it to your life. I encourage you to read the text Mark 4:1–20 each day, asking God to let you hear what this parable is saying to you. "He, who has ears to hear, let him hear." Remember the disciples who walked with Jesus everyday couldn't understand it, so be careful not to be over confident that you know what this parable is saying to you today.

THE SEED AND THE SOIL– THE WAYSIDE SOIL

MARK 4:1–20

We continue our look at "The Seed and the Soil." I am asking you to re-read our text and ask yourself which soil am I. Better yet, ask the Holy Spirit to show you which soil you are in this parable. Remember the bottom line of this parable is this: The seed is the Word of God and the soil is your heart and life. How can you tell which soil is the condition of your heart? Dare I say we all may have a bit of each soil in our lives but seek to know which one is the most prevalent?

WAYSIDE SOIL

> And these are the ones by the wayside where the word is sown. When they hear, Satan comes immediately and takes away the word that was sown in their hearts.
>
> Mark 4:15 (NKJV)

THE BUZZARD IS PERCHED IN THE TREE

The devil knows how powerful the Word of God is and how much fruit it will bear if placed upon fertile soil. He is like a bird perched in the tree waiting to swoop down and steal the Word that has been sown into your life before it can begin to take root.

He swoops down with doubt. He swoops down with fear. He swoops down with our past. He swoops down with pride. He swoops down with sin. He swoops down with unworthiness. He swoops down with distractions, etc.

THINK OF ALL THAT'S BEEN STOLEN!

How many miracles have been stolen from us because the soil of our hearts was wayside and unprotected by our faith? How much improvement of life have we missed because the soil of our hearts was wayside? How much unnecessary struggle have we wrestled with because the soil of our hearts has been wayside?

PRACTICAL APPLICATION AND CHALLENGE

Ask the Holy Spirit to plow the soil of your heart so it will be fertile to receive the seed of God's Word and produce its life and life more abundantly fruit. Guard the Word of God that has been sown into your life. Don't let the devil swoop down and steal it, because he's perched right now to swoop down if you'll let him. Ask the Holy Spirit to show you what to do to shoo the devil away from stealing the seeds of God's Word into you life.

THE SEED AND THE SOIL—
SHALLOW GROUND

MARK 4:1–20

We continue our look at "The Seed and the Soil." I am asking you to reread our text and ask yourself, "Which soil am I?" Better yet, ask the Holy Spirit to show you which soil you are in this parable. Remember the bottom line of this parable is this: The seed is the Word of God and the soil is your heart and life.

> Some fell on stony ground, where it did not have much earth; and immediately it sprang up because it had no depth of earth. ⁶But when the sun was up it was scorched, and because it had no root it withered away.
>
> Mark 4:5–6 (NKJV)

These likewise are the ones sown on stony ground who, when they hear the word, immediately receive it with gladness; ¹⁷and they have no root in themselves, and so endure only for a time. Afterward, when tribulation or persecution arises for the word's sake, immediately they stumble.

Mark 4:16–17 (NKJV)

OUT OF THE GATE WIDE OPEN!

The cheetah is the fastest land mammal with speeds of up to seventy miles an hour! The only problem is, it cannot sustain that for very long. The reason is, he has a small heart incapable of continuing to pump the blood to supply the muscles. Sadly, I have seen many receive Christ or return to Christ and come out of the gate running wide open, only to see them wither within a short time.

WHY?

Why do they spring up so fast and seem to be making such good progress, only to fall when the heat of life comes down on them? In the parable, the soil is not very deep, so it only has one way to go, up. The new convert or prodigal that has come home is running on many emotions, which is great, but they need to take the time to develop some faith and deeper soil.

AN INDICTMENT!

Ultimately, the individual is responsible for how deep they develop their faith, but I must also lay a partial indictment at the feet of the church and Christians in general, including myself.

Jesus' command was to go and make disciples, not converts. Salvation in Christ is simply the gateway to new life, but discipleship is the pathway to sustaining new life.

HOW DOES ONE DEVELOP DEEPER FAITH?

First, it takes time. The depth of our overall faith is in proportion to the depth of our relationship with God. It is out of your relationship with God that your faith grows. A growing relationship with God includes the following:

1–Spending time with Him in prayer and communion.

2–Spending time in His Word.

3–Living in simple obedience to His Word in all areas of your life.

Also, be apart of an accountable relationship with a Christian whose faith is deeper than yours. Ask them the questions on how to overcome the trials of life and allow them to speak into your life.

CHALLENGE

How deep is your soil? Are you cultivating your faith to be deeper faith? Do you know someone whose faith is withering away? Can you help them by showing them how to develop a deeper faith?

The Seed and the Soil– Thorny Ground

Mark 4:1–20

We continue our look at "The Seed and the Soil." I am asking you to re-read our text and ask yourself, "Which soil am I?" Better yet, ask the Holy Spirit to show you which soil you are in this parable. Remember the bottom line of this parable is this: The seed is the Word of God and the soil is your heart and life.

> And some *seed* fell among thorns; and the thorns grew up and choked it, and it yielded no crop.
>
> Mark 4:7 (NKJV)

> Now these are the ones sown among thorns; *they are* the ones who hear the word, ¹⁹and the cares of this world, the deceitfulness of riches, and the desires for other things entering in choke the word, and it becomes unfruitful.
>
> Mark 4:18–19 (NKJV)

The Soil of Most American Christians

Sadly, this is where I see many Christians today—in the thorny soil. Notice what the text said, it was alive but unfruitful. How tragic and miserable such a life is. Always struggling and encumbered about in life knowing you should be enjoying life but are not.

Notice the 3 types of thorns: cares of this world, deceitfulness of riches, desire for other things.

Cares of This World

This could include anxiety, bitterness, un-forgiveness, pride, striving to climb the ladder, etc...Jesus said not to worry but seek first the Kingdom of God and its righteousness and all your needs will be supplied.

Deceitfulness of Riches

God never said that it was a sin to have riches, but it is a sin for riches to have you. The Rich Young ruler that came to Jesus was a man owned by riches. We see that because when Jesus challenged him to sell all he had, give it to the poor, take up his cross and follow Jesus, he went away sad. He went away sad because riches owned him. Admit it or not, we've all had to or are dealing with this fruit-choking weed in our life. You will work extended periods of time, miss church for extended periods of time, compromise your devotional time, etc. All to make money to support a standard of living that you want. Sounds like the deceitfulness of riches.

Desire for Other Things

God doesn't banish desires; he just wants them in line with His Word and Will. "If I could just have that job I would be happy. If I could have that car; that house; those clothes; that person, then I'd be happy." Those are desires for other things and they are choking the fruit capacity out of the

Word of God. This is the sad state of that poor soul, who tries to have the world and Christ too. You know that you should be living sold out to Christ, but you will not let go of your desires for "stuff." (Read Prov 3:1–10.)

The Word of God is powerful and when it is sown into your life, its purpose is to produce fruit in your life. To produce the fruit of joy, peace, fulfillment, satisfaction, etc. However, the soil has to be good soil or else you are going to be very frustrated knowing that you should be fruitful but indeed are barren. To be alive but fruitless, what a horrible place to be.

CHALLENGE

Does this describe the soil of your heart? If so what do you do?

Heb 12:1–2 and Matt 6:33 gives the answer. Repent, deal with the issues, unshackle yourself from the cares of this world, seek first the Kingdom of God's success above your own, and set your desire on Christ.

THE SEED AND THE SOIL–
GOOD GROUND
VARIED GROWTH

MARK 4:1–20

Today we come to the last analogy of the various soils that
the seed could lie in.

> But other *seed* fell on good ground and yielded
> a crop that sprang up, increased and produced:
> some thirtyfold, some sixty, and some a
> hundred.
>
> Mark 4:8 (NKJV)

> But these are the ones sown on good ground,
> those who hear the word, accept *it,* and bear
> fruit: some thirtyfold, some sixty, and some a
> hundred.
>
> Mark 4:20 (NKJV)

ACCEPT IT

First I must qualify what Jesus meant when he said, "accept it."

> Therefore whoever hears these sayings of mine, and does them, I will liken him to a wise man who built his house on the rock:
>
> Matt 7:24 (NKJV)

> But everyone who hears these sayings of mine, and does not do them, will be like a foolish man who built his house on the sand:
>
> Matt 7:26 (NKJV)

To accept the Word, you must believe it and you don't really believe it unless you act upon it. Simply hearing the Word is not enough to activate its power and potential in your life; you must act upon it.

WHY THIRTY, SIXTY AND ONE HUNDRED?

There's a question as of to why some produced thirty some sixty and some one hundred. Why didn't all of them produce one hundred? What determines the ability is not in the seed but in the soil. All the potential for a hundred fold is in every seed. The soil in which the seed resides determines if the seed will be allowed to reach its fullest potential. The deeper your faith, the more fruit the Word is going to have in your life. Please refer to the devotional *Genuine Faith–Part 2* on how to deepen your faith.

Rejoice over the fact that the Word of God is producing thirty fold in your life, but deepen your faith and you'll see the Word produce even more in your life. Don't allow the cares of this life to come in and begin to choke out what the

Word is producing in your life. Remember the deeper you go the more you grow.

WHICH SOIL ARE YOU REALLY?

So which soil are you? If you are frustrated over the fact that you don't see the Word producing more fruit in your life, don't be frustrated with God, examine the soil of your life.

I leave you with a great promise God said about His Word. This Scripture tells you what His intentions are about His Word and what you can expect His Word to do if you'll go deeper.

> So shall My word be that goes forth from My mouth; It shall not return to Me void, But it shall accomplish what I please, And it shall prosper in the thing for which I sent it.
>
> Isa 55:11 (NKJV)

THE DEVIL HAS PLANS– PART 1

JOHN 10:10; 2 COR 2:11; EPH 6:12

First Church was experiencing what some would call a revival. Sinners were receiving Christ as their LORD and Savior. People were being filled with the Holy Spirit. Broken marriages were being put back together. Those bound by addictions were being set free. Believers were actively engaged in ministry both within and without the four walls of the church building. They were not just having church, they were being the church.

THE MEETING

In the regions of darkness, two of Satan's commanding officers, Clem and Doby, who had been sent to destroy the First Church, had been summoned by Satan to give a report of their progress. As they waited outside, they were discussing how they were going to tell their boss the bad news. The door opened to Satan's chamber and Satan's foul stench of violence and hate smote Clem and Doby with fear and trembling. "Come," said Satan.

They swallowed hard and sheepishly entered Satan's chamber. "So how goes your work at the First Church congregation?"

BAD NEWS, BAD RESPONSE

Clem and Doby fell down at his feet begging for mercy. As they began to relay what was going on at the First Church congregation Satan's face boiled with rage and anger. The devil was absolutely livid over the progress the First Church was making. His head reeled in pain at the reports of the congregation growing and touching people's lives with the gospel of Christ. He loathed the unity in that congregation. He was sickened when He heard believers were forgiving one another and working together for the cause of Christ.

The regions of darkness trembled when Satan let out a roar of anger towards Clem and Doby.

"You fools! I ought to throw you into the abyss myself! I sent you to destroy that congregation but under your watch it's becoming a nightmare for me!"

"Master you must do something and do it fast!" said Clem.

"Yeah, all the demons in the region refuse to work with us because it's too hazardous for their health," said Doby.

"I'll be hazardous to your health!" roared Satan.

"Sir if you don't act fast and come up with a plan, we'll never stop them!" stammered Clem.

THE DEVIL HAS PLANS ALRIGHT

"Oh, I've got plans for that congregation all right," said the devil. "Go look in my special bag of tricks over there and fetch me a plan with the ultimate weapon that I can use to destroy this nemesis congregation."

With an evil, expecting chuckle, Clem made his way to the bag. He opened it and pulled out what appeared to be a set of plans. "Here they are your evilness."

The Devil Unfurled the Plans on the Table.

"Ahh yes, the plan of distraction and discouragement to keep them from praying. Oh, this one has saved a many a demon from pain and agony. This is one my most important plans, because it causes Christians and the congregation to stymie and become lethargic. It has put many a congregation into religious sleep and has caused people to live in their bondage."

"But that's not going to bust up this congregation. I want something that is going to tear that congregation to shreds. I want something that is brutally cruel and will inflict the most damage, something that will cause believers to walk away from Christ all together. Something that will damn souls to hell! Go get me another plan!"

Are You A Victim of This Plan?

The prayerless believer is one that is weak, anemic, and lulled into a spiritual slumber. A prayerless saint and congregation are of no threat to the devil or his kingdom. Nevertheless, a greater loss of being a prayerless saint is you miss out on the blessings of God's communion and fellowship. You miss the joy and strength of His presence. You miss the victories that Christ secured at the cross for you. You miss rescuing others from the clutches of spiritual darkness. You miss so many of the blessings that God has for His children on this side of heaven.

Indeed, one of the devil's plans to destroy your life and the life of any congregation is that of distraction and discouragement to pray. Have you fallen for this plan? The longer his plan has been at work in your life and the life of a congregation, the harder it is to break free. If you find it difficult, pray and confess to God that you've fallen prey to the devil's plan and begin to cry out to God to deliver you.

The devil's Ultimate Plan

Although this plan of distraction and discouragement is a power plan, this is not the devil's most effective weapon. So what is the devil's most effective weapon that will inflict the most harm and damage in your life and that of a church congregation? I want something that will shred lives and cause people to walk away from Christ altogether. I have seen it myself and indeed, it is the most hideous plan I have ever seen. Perhaps our next time together the devil will reveal it.

THE DEVIL HAS PLANS– PART 2

I JOHN 4:1–3; I TIM 4:1–3; I TIM 6:3–5;
2 COR 11:13–15

We continue to look in on a meeting between Satan and two of his commanders, Clem and Doby. First Church congregation is experiencing what many would call a revival. The devil is searching for the most hideous and scrupulous plan, which will tear that congregation apart and cause many to walk away from Christ. The first plan they looked at was discouragement and distraction to pray. Although powerful, that was not the plan the devil had in mind.

> Now the Spirit expressly says that in latter times, some will depart from the faith, giving heed to deceiving spirits and doctrines of demons.
>
> I Tim 4:1 (NKJV)

Another Destructive Plan

"Bring me another plan, one that will indeed cut the spiritual throat of that congregation!" snarled the devil.

Doby rushed over to Satan's bag of tricks and dug around until he found what he thought for sure would do the trick.

"Here your evilness, I'm sure this one will do the trick."

"Ahhhhh yessss" hissed Satan, "Doubting the Word of God." Oh, this is a good one. All I have to do is plant some of my double agents in there to begin to logically, yet oh so subtly bring about questions to the Bible. Questions like, 'If Adam and Eve were the only people on the planet and they had Cain and Able, where did Cain's wife come from?' Oh yes this is too good! Then I begin to sprinkle more and more doubts and incite endless debate and questioning that they cannot give answers to. This will lead them to call into question their beliefs and voila! But wait a minute! You guys told me that the majority of the congregation was baptized in the Holy Spirit!"

Clem and Doby shook their heads saying, "Yeah with all that un-tie my bow-tie re-tie my bow-tie speaking in tongues stuff!" said Clem "Yeah it's enough to give you a migraine!" said Doby.

"Then this plan will not work so well on the congregation because the Holy Spirit is a revealer of truth. Once the Holy Spirit reveals the truth to them, they will not fall for this plan! *Arrg*! Get me another plan, *now*!" roared Satan.

> However, when He, the Spirit of truth, has come, He will guide you into all truth; for He will not speak on His own authority, but whatever He hears He will speak; and He will tell you things to come. ¹⁴He will glorify Me, for He will take of what is Mine and declare it to you.
>
> John 16:13–14 (NKJV)

Doubting or Perverting the Word of God

There is no doubt that Satan is constantly trying to bring doubt into the minds of God's people. There are many "scholars" of religion who are used by Satan to bring "logical" doubt to the Word of God. There are without a doubt many "logical" questions that lead to no answers, just aimless debate. Jesus said unless you have the faith of a child you will by no means enter into heaven. The faith of a child is "pure" and "simple." In fact, it is that kind of faith that Jesus said would move mountains.

So when you feel this plan of the devil being exacted into your life, fall back to the simple faith in God and His Word. Rely on the Holy Spirit to reveal truth and lies. The Bible warns us that in the "Last Days," meaning the time between the cross and the rapture, many false prophets and doctrines of demons will be unleashed on this world. Therefore, we must be steadfast in the simple faith and not allow ourselves to be drawn into Satan's plan to cause you to doubt God's Word.

> But evil men and impostors will grow worse and worse, deceiving and being deceived. [14]But you must continue in the things which you have learned and been assured of, knowing from whom you have learned them, [15]and that from childhood you have known the Holy Scriptures, which are able to make you wise for salvation through faith which is in Christ Jesus.
>
> 2 Tim 3:13–15 (NKJV)

The Ultimate Plan

Although there have been congregations, and indeed whole denominations, which have strayed from the truth of God's Word, this plan is not the devil's most destructive one

People have been ripped to shreds by his most destructive plan. Adults, youth, and kids have been affected by it and sadly, many have walked away from Christ altogether and are now in hell because of it. So what is it? Perhaps our next time together the devil will reveal it.

THE DEVIL HAS PLANS–
PART 3

REV 2:1–5; MARK 12:30

We continue looking in on a conversation between Satan and two of his commanders, Clem and Doby, who were supposed to be in charge of the destruction of the First Church congregation. Yet the congregation is experiencing life as a true New Testament Church. This has the devil fuming and seeking through his plans to find the ultimate plan that will bring about hideous results. But he's also looking for one that will bring these deadly spiritual results quickly. He has looked at two plans and although they are plans he uses to bring down Christians and congregations, they are not what he's looking for.

ONE OF THE BETTER ONES INDEED

"Get me another plan you idiots!" Clem and Doby both scurried over to Satan's bag of tricks and dug around until they found one that looked promising from its title, "Lost

Love For Jesus." They both looked at each other, simultaneously grinned and scurried over to satan.

"Here's one your evilness, 'Lost Love For Jesus.'" They all shuddered when they mentioned the name of "Jesus."

"Ah Yes," Satan said, slightly lifting his head, gazing off in a stare as he reflected upon this plan's effectiveness. "This is a good one ... in fact it's one of my better ones. I have taken many a Christian and congregation out with this one. They don't even see it coming."

"Oh good boss, tell us how the plan works," said Clem.

"Yeah tell us. We want to take them out!" said Doby.

"The first thing you have to do is back off from frontal attacks."

"What! Don't attack! What kind of a plan is this?" exclaimed Clem and Doby.

AN UNUSUAL PLAN OF ATTACK

"When a Christian or congregation is red hot in love with Je-Je-Je, well you know who, they are used to the frontal attacks, and because of those attacks they cling closely to Je-Je-Je-. So after a while you back off on the frontal attacks to put them at ease. Simultaneously you subtly begin to convince them that all is well, to relax a little and start enjoying life. Of course, they will argue that they are not going to compromise their doctrine or good works. Oh no they can keep their doctrine, in fact encourage them to talk about it more among themselves."

"What! Are you kidding us?" said Clem.

"Oh no," said the devil, "You keep them focused on their doctrine. All along you convince them that because they hold such a high standard of doctrine and everyone knows it, they can relax a bit on their prayer life and Bible study. They know what they believe, no need to keep reading the same thing over and over. They know who Je- Je- Je- is and are convinced they know him well, so no need to pray as much."

"As they begin to relax in their personal prayer and Bible study, they begin to lose strength. They will notice it, so you point them to their beliefs and doctrine. Your goal is to get them believing in something they are not practicing any more. You get them depending on defending their doctrinal purity to soothe their religious conscience. Before you know it, they will have lost their first love for, well you know who."

"Ahhhhhhhh!" said Clem and Doby.

BUT WAIT A MINUTE

The devil stared off with a face of satisfaction on this plan, when suddenly his expression changed as a thought raced through his mind.

"But wait a minute!" said the devil, "We don't have that kind of time, because this plan takes years to accomplish, although it is deadly indeed. I want a plan that is the fastest and most devastating plan I have in my arsenal. I want one that will spread like wild fire, consume everyone in its wake, and leave that congregation in ashes. I want one that is going to have the highest spiritual mortality rate. I want one that is going to gouge their hearts out! I want to make them pay dearly for what they've done to my kingdom! Go get me another plan you bumbling idiots! *Now!*" he said, as he pounded the table.

HAVE YOU LEFT YOUR FIRST LOVE FOR JESUS?

Are you truly in love with Jesus or are you just going through the motions of what you believe? You may attend church and defend your doctrinal beliefs to a tee. You may be well versed in what you believe and may even point out the false errors of other's teachings. But are you in love with Jesus?

How do you know if you're in love with Jesus? Do you have a desire to pray? Do you have a desire to read the Bible as if it's a letter from Jesus to you? Are you defending doctrinal purity because you love Jesus or because it soothes your religious conscience? Are you practicing what you say you believe? Is your heart stirred with longing desire to be in His presence? Read our text Rev 2:1–5.

THE WORST IS YET TO COME

Although this plan is truly one of the devil's most effective plans and countless believers and congregations have fallen victim to it, it is not his most hideous plan in his bag of tricks. Again, I tell you I have seen it and it truly is merciless and brutal. I have watched in horror as believers and congregations have been devoured spiritually by it. Perhaps our next time together the devil will finally unveil this hideous plan.

THE DEVIL HAS PLANS–
PART 4

2 COR 3:4–18; JOHN 16:13–15; 1 COR 2:9–14;
LUKE 24:46–49

We join in on the growing intensity of the conversation between Satan and two of his commanders, Clem and Doby. Clem and Doby were sent to destroy the congregation at First Church. Rather than destruction, the congregation is experiencing growth, not just numerically but spiritually as well. People are being saved and lives are being changed. The pastor of the congregation, William Smith, has been guiding the congregation through the assaults of darkness.

THE DEVIL SEARCHES

The devil, frustrated with Clem and Doby's ability to find a most affective plan to destroy First Church congregation, goes himself to his bag of tricks to find one. Vengeance and violence fills the room as the devil rummages around in his bag, mumbling curses under his breath at First Church congregation.

He finds one, lays it aside, continues to rummage through the bag, and finds another. He then brings both plans to the table and unfurls them.

A DOUBLE WHAMMY

"This congregation is so strong I need to combine two plans into one. I will attack the baptism of the Holy Spirit and their focus on their mission."

"Attack the baptism of the Holy Spirit! How are you going to do that?" exclaimed Doby.

"Yeah, all that un-tie my bow-tie, re-tie my bow-tie speaking in tongues stuff sends all the demons reeling in confusion!" said Clem.

"I'll give you ear plugs and a promise to send you to the abyss if you foul it up!" said Satan. Clem and Doby took a hard gulp.

SELF-CENTERED PENTECOSTALISM

"We want the congregation and believers to make the baptism of the Holy Spirit and the gifts of the Spirit an emotional experience as an end unto itself. We want them to purely emotionalize everything about the Holy Spirit. This will cause them to seek emotionalism in every worship service and that alone. We'll tell them 'you're having church now because you feel something.'"

"But what about all that speaking in tongues stuff, won't that bring down the heat on us?" asked Clem.

"Yeah you've got to take the heat, but you keep them focused on seeking the emotions and get them wrapped up in the emotions alone and before too long, it'll be a self-centered Pentecost. This leads them right into the second plan, loss of focus on their mission."

"When you get a self-centered Pentecostal church, they get all wrapped up in the 'feel good,' 'what's in it for me' emotions and forget all about what they're supposed to be doing. They become a 'secret little club.' You convince them to be proud of the fact that they are a small congregation because they are Pentecostal. You need to make them suspicious of all visitors in that they have come to spy on them and dilute their 'Pentecostal experience.'"

RESULTS OF SELF-CENTERED PENTECOSTALISM

"Oh I get it," exclaimed Doby. "When you get them all wrapped up in emotionalism they forget why they received the baptism of the Holy Spirit to begin with!"

"Boy that'll be a relief!" said Clem. "When they forget that the baptism of the Holy Spirit was to empower them to live right and give them supernatural power to be a witness for Christ, they are essentially no longer a threat to us."

"Now you're getting it," said Satan. "Now you boys take these plans the legion of demons in that area and strike with a vengeance."

Clem and Doby took the plans and gloated with sinister chuckles. As they were making their way out the door the devil interrupted their gloating. "Hold it ... hold it ... hold it. Those plans won't work either," Satan said with disgust.

"Why not boss?" they said.

PROTECTION AGAINST SUCH PLANS

"It will not work because their pastor is William Smith." Clem and Doby shuttered at the mention of Pastor Smith.

"He's been burned by these plans before and is aware that we are planning such an attack and that's why he's so big into discipleship. Discipleship brings a balance to the experiential aspects of the Spirit. It would take a long time to enact these plans with any success if we were to gain any at all."

"*Argg*! There's got to a plan that can break into this congregation! There's got to be something that I can use to bust them up!" Suddenly the devil stopped with a thought of inspiration expressed upon his face and His eyes shifted back and forth. "By devil I've got it!" In puzzled awe and wonder, he sat down, "by devil I've got it!"

The Devil's Ultimate Plan

We'll have to wait until our next time together to see the devil's most hideous and ultimate plan to destroy First Church congregation.

Are You Entrapped?

If you are a Pentecostal, have you been entrapped with the devil's plan to make it a self-seeking experience? Is your faith in God more based upon your emotions and the way you feel or from the Word of God being instilled in your soul? Is your mission to "experience" the Holy Spirit at the worship service and live week to week with that being your primary mission?

Yes, enjoy the experience of the supernatural presence of God through Holy Spirit. Be refreshed by it, be empowered by it, but don't lose sight that the primary reason for Baptism of the Holy Spirit is for empowerment to *be* a witness in lifestyle and tongue.

> But you shall receive power when the Holy Spirit
> has come upon you; and you shall be witnesses to
> Me in Jerusalem, and in all Judea and Samaria,
> and to the end of the earth.
>
> Acts 1:8 (NKJV)

THE DEVIL HAS PLANS–
PART 5

SCRIPTURES CONTAINED WITHIN
THE DEVOTIONAL

THE DEVIL'S NEMESIS–FIRST
CHURCH CONGREGATION

We have been watching the conversation between the devil and two of his commanders, Clem and Doby. Clem and Doby were sent by Satan to destroy the congregation at First Church. First Church has been seeing sinners saved and prodigals come back home to God every week. They have seen marriages that were on the brink of divorce, reconciled. Why, they've even seen couples that had been divorced be reconciled and remarried to each other. Scores of believers are being baptized in the Holy Spirit. The youth group is reaching dozens and dozens of their lost classmates for Christ. Even the kid's ministries are seeing a move of God. It's just phenomenal what God is doing in and through the congregation at First Church. It would seem that First Church was immune to any device or plan of the devil.

Now the devil has some hideous plans of destruction for believers and congregations. Nevertheless, the one he's about to unleash on the congregation at First Church is by far the most cruel and devastating of them all. If effective in the First Church congregation, many will walk away from Christ and many lives will be absolutely devastated. Is there anything this congregation can do to stop this plan from being successful?

THE DEVIL'S ULTIMATE PLAN

"By devil that's it!" exclaimed the devil. "Why didn't I think of this one before? It's perfect! I've destroyed more churches, especially strong ones, with this plan than any other plan I have. The bonus of this plan is that once it's started it spreads rapidly, like wild fire, throughout the whole congregation."

"What is it boss?" said Clem

"Oh this is too good," said the devil. "This one plan has ripped the hearts out of so many people. It has caused countless people to walk away from church and God, more than any other plan. It has injured and spiritually maimed so many. It has driven many a minister out of the ministry altogether. It has split more churches, more families, more marriages, and more friendships; oh it's so good because it leaves such devastation in its wake!"

"What is it boss, what is it?" exclaimed Doby

"My most hideous plan that causes such mass devastation is … the tongue."

THE PLAN REVEALED

> And the tongue is a fire, a world of iniquity.
> The tongue is so set among our members that
> it defiles the whole body, and sets on fire the
> course of nature; and it is set on fire by hell.
>
> James 3:6 (NKJV)

What Fuels The Tongue?

What fuels the tongue to be such an instrument of Satan? Don't think for a moment that you are too holy and righteous to fall for this plan of the devil. If you think you are, then you've already fallen for it. The fuel of the tongue is within your heart.

> A good man out of the good treasure of his heart brings forth good; and an evil man out of the evil treasure of his heart brings forth evil. For out of the abundance of the heart his mouth speaks.
>
> Luke 6:45 (NKJV)

It's sad but painfully true that many have been spiritually wounded and some mortally through the tongue of a "believer." Yet the tongue is only an instrument of the heart. Believers are to guard their hearts, because we have within us all an ally for the devil, our Adamic nature. Through Christ, we do not have to yield to it, but you will have to battle it. When we get our focus on *self*, we have just awakened the devil's ally within us. He will pour on the fuel of jealousy and envy. He will fan the flames of your selfishness, what I want, my rights, my way, me, me, me, me.

Yet, those whose tongue is being used by the devil do not realize it or if they do, will deny it or at the very least, not acknowledge such.

> Who is wise and understanding among you? (Who says they are spiritual and doing right?) Let him show by good conduct that his works are done in the meekness of wisdom. 14But if you have bitter envy and self-seeking in your hearts, do not boast and lie against the truth. 15This wisdom does not descend from above, but is earthly, sensual, demonic. 16For

where envy and self-seeking exist, confusion and every evil thing are there. ¹⁷But the wisdom that is from above is first pure, then peaceable, gentle, willing to yield, full of mercy and good fruits, without partiality and without hypocrisy. ¹⁸Now the fruit of righteousness is sown in peace by those who make peace.

James 3:13–18 (NKJV)

Don't think the devil doesn't believe in the scriptures. He knows the power of the tongue and he's intent on tapping into his ally within you. The devil wants to use your tongue to bring death and destruction to believers and the church.

Words kill, words give life; they're either poison or fruit—you choose.

Prov 18:21 (MSG)

ARE YOU BEING USED BY THE DEVIL?

Is the devil using your tongue to bring death? Are your words tearing down others in your congregation? Are you upset because you didn't get your way or you feel offended? If so, are you going to others with your offense to gain allies to your cause? Are you tearing down those who have "offended" you with your tongue before others? When someone comes to you with words that accuse and tear down others, do you agree with them or worse yet, repeat the same?

Search your heart for any bitterness, unforgiveness, offence, etc., because that is fuel for the tongue. These things bring nothing but destruction to you and those around you.

Look after each other so that not one of you will fail to find God's best blessings. Watch out that no bitterness takes root among you, for as it springs up it causes deep trouble, hurting many in their spiritual lives.

Heb 12:15 (TLB)

In the Church, there is a right way and a wrong way to confront wrongs. Unfortunately, the majority of the time, the wrong way is used. The wrong way is all based on *self*. The right way is all based on *Christ*. We will look at the right way our next time together.

WHAT TO DO?

If the devil has used your tongue to inflict injury to others, then repent, go to God and ask for forgiveness, and ask Him to reveal and remove the roots of bitterness that are fueling your tongue. Then, if possible, you should go to those whom your tongue has brought injury, ask for forgiveness, and seek to be reconciled with them.

Don't allow the devil to use his ultimate plan in your life or the life of your congregation.

The Antidote For
the Devil's Ultimate Plan.

James 3

Did his Plan Work?

Did the congregation of First Church fall prey to the devil's ultimate plan of destruction? Well, because this was a fable, it remains to be seen, because this fable could be any congregation in the world. Although there are many, many other plans the devil has in his bag of tricks, this one plan of the tongue seems to be his deadliest. So how do you guard yourself and the congregation you're a part of from this plan being enacted and stopped if enacted?

Does He Have an Ally in You?

First remember that the devil has an ally in us all, the Adamic nature. As a Christian, we are to keep it subdued by the power of Christ. That power is the Word and the Spirit. We engage that power through simple obedience. You must be a student of the Word coupled with being a person of prayer and communion with God. You must keep your heart open and tender before God.

This is how I pray in regards to offenses. When it comes to offenses done to me, I pray that my heart will be as an oily flint rock and that the offenses will roll right off and not stick. However, when it comes to offending God, I pray that my heart will be sensitive to the slightest offense and respond immediately to the Spirit's conviction.

WHAT'S AT THE CENTER OF HIS PLAN?

Remember that at the center of this ultimate plan of the devil is selfishness.

> For where envy and self-seeking exist, confusion
> and every evil thing are there.
>
> James 3:16 (NKJV)

If there is confusion within a congregation you can know that *self-seeking* is at the root of it all. However, it's not advertised as such, but rather it is advertised as what is *"right."* That's why the Bible says:

> Who is wise and understanding among you? Let
> him show by good conduct that his works are
> done in the meekness of wisdom. ¹⁴But if you
> have bitter envy and self-seeking in your hearts,
> do not boast and lie against the truth. ¹⁵This
> wisdom does not descend from above, but is
> earthly, sensual, demonic. ¹⁶For where envy
> and self-seeking exist, confusion and every evil
> thing are there.
>
> James 3:13–16 (NKJV)

Look at what the Bible says is true wisdom within the congregation:

> But the wisdom that is from above is first pure,
> then peaceable, gentle, willing to yield, full
> of mercy and good fruits, without partiality
> and without hypocrisy. [18]Now the fruit of
> righteousness is sown in peace by those who
> make peace.
>
> James 3:17–18 (NKJV)

I LOVE YOU BUT YOU GET ON MY NERVES!

As Christians, we are going to have times when we get on each other's nerves, so to speak. There are going to be times when we are genuinely offended. We are still human and will continue to be such until death or rapture. So, in the meantime, this is how God says we are to handle offenses and dealings with each other. The Bible also shows us that we have an obligation to pursue peace and unity within the congregation.

> Therefore, as the elect of God, holy and beloved,
> put on tender mercies, kindness, humility,
> meekness, longsuffering; [13]bearing with one
> another, and forgiving one another, if anyone
> has a complaint against another; even as Christ
> forgave you, so you also must do. [14]But above all
> these things put on love, which is the bond of
> perfection. [15]And let the peace of God rule in
> your hearts, to which also you were called in one
> body; and be thankful.
>
> Col 3:12–15 (NKJV)

> I, therefore, the prisoner of the LORD, beseech
> you to walk worthy of the calling with which you
> were called, [2]with all lowliness and gentleness,

with longsuffering, bearing with one another in love, ³endeavoring to keep the unity of the Spirit in the bond of peace.

Eph 4:1–3 (NKJV)

WATCH OVER & RESCUE THEM IF POSSIBLE

Do you know someone that is caught up in the devil's ultimate plan? Do you know someone that is causing confusion in a congregation? The longer a person is trapped in Satan's plan it is usually harder for them to realize it. The best thing is to heed the warning and admonition of the Word:

> Look after each other so that not one of you will fail to find God's best blessings. Watch out that no bitterness takes root among you, for as it springs up it causes deep trouble, hurting many in their spiritual lives.
>
> Heb 12:15 (TLB)

STAND UP TO THE DEVIL

Stand up to the devil's plan for your life and the life of the congregation you are a part of. If by the grace of God, you realize that *you* have fallen prey to the devil's plan, you need to repent. Be aware that your selfishness and pride will fight bitterly to keep you from doing such. However, to be set free from the selfishness and bitterness, you must openly and completely repent before God. Once you've done that, you need to go to those whom you have spoken against and ask them to forgive you and seek to be reconciled with them.

If one that you are close to in relationship is falling prey to this plan, remember you have a responsibility to "look after each other so that not one of you will fail to find God's best blessings."

Faithful are the wounds of a friend, but the kisses of an enemy are deceitful.

Prov 27:6 (NKJV)

The Straggler

1 Pet 5:8; Heb 10:23–25; Eccl 4:9–10, 12

The Baby Zebra

From the time he was born, it was drilled into him to stick with the group. Everywhere they went they always went as a group. He was always stuck in the middle of the group when they went galloping from one feeding ground to another. Being in the middle of a galloping group has several disadvantages. For one, you're always eating dust, because being in the middle of the pack the dust has nowhere to go but in your mouth and up your nose. Another is you cannot see where you're going, just use your imagination a little to imagine the view from being in the middle of the pack.

Stick With The Group!

At every stop, it was drilled into him, "stick with the group." He was sick and tired of sticking with the group. He wanted to venture out on his own a little, get some of that greener grass out there away from the group. As he would start to stray from the group one would say, "Stick with the pack," and he'd draw back closer to the pack. It seemed that someone from the group was always watching when he tried to slip away for just a few bites of that tall greener grass just a few hundred yards away.

THE GREENER GRASS

One day, he'd had enough. That green grass was just too green and too plentiful to pass up. As he started towards the tall greener grass, one from the group said, "Stick with the pack," but he paid no attention to their call. As he kept trotting off, another from the groups said, "Stick with the pack, it's safe here." Safe, he thought, trying running behind your ... well it's not the best view in the safari. Other's began to call out to him, "Don't stray from the pack, stay with us it's safer." What's with all this "safer" stuff, there's no lions around here?

As he trotted over to the tall green grass, the closer he got the better it looked. It was much taller than the grass the pack was scrounging up. It was thicker too. He trotted up to it and began to munch on the outer parameter of this oasis of grass. The pack stayed where they where. He stood there looking over his shoulder at them thinking what fools they are. It's much easier to find the food you want if no one is around to tell you what to do.

A MEETING OF THE EYES

As he bent down to munch on another mouth full of this luscious grass, his eyes met another set of eyes. He froze in fear, not believing what was seeing staring back at him. It was the eyes of a lion. With a tremendous burst of energy, the lion sprang from its hiding place in the tall green grass. When that first lion sprang into action, a couple of others hidden in the tall grass sprang into action as well. The young zebra was now running for his life. The pack quickly huddled up and ran from the threat. Well you know what happened, a tragic end.

A Real Adversary

The Bible says that Satan is like a lion seeking whom he may devour. In the animal kingdom, a lion typically will not attack the group, they attack those that stray from the safety of the group. So it is with spiritual life of believers. If you stray from the group, you are easy prey for the devil and he will devour you spiritually.

As a pastor, I've seen it time and time again. People find all kinds of excuses of slip away from church attendance, fellowship, etc … and I've heard countless excuses to justify slipping away from the pack. I'm not just talking about the "babes in Christ," I'm talking about those that have been Christians for years. Yet, without fail, before too long, the devil, that lion seeking whom he may devour, attacks and devours them spiritually. I've seen family devoured, children devoured, finances devoured, health devoured … all because they strayed away from the "pack."

Responsibility

> Brethren, if anyone among you wanders from the truth, and someone turns him back, ²⁰let him know that he who turns a sinner from the error of his way will save a soul from death and cover a multitude of sins.
>
> James 5:19–20 (NKJV)

Are you warning and reaching out to those that are beginning to stray from the "pack." Don't think that it's the "pastor's" job to reach all those that are straying from the "pack"; for you have responsibility for your "brother" as well. Why are they straying? Is it because they don't feel welcomed in the "pack?" Is it because they don't see the value of being a part of the "pack"? Are you reaching out to those that are and have strayed from the "pack"? You cannot force someone to be a part if they don't want to, but you need to try.

If you haven't been devoured yet, you will be. You may be devoured by the poisoned venom of deceit into thinking that you're life is really no different than when you were with the "pack." Unlike the unfortunate zebra in our story, if you find yourself being devoured, you can call upon Jesus to rescue you from the jaws of Satan. If you're life has become a shambles from being devoured, you can still go to Jesus and He can give you new life.

Don't stray from the "pack" because it's safer. Well what about the injuries one receives from being in the "pack"? That will be our next time together. However, in a healthy "pack," there is safety, so don't stray from the "pack."

> Be sober, be vigilant; because your adversary the devil walks about like a roaring lion, seeking whom he may devour.
>
> 1 Pet 5:8 (NKJV)

COMING BACK TO THE PACK

GAL 6:1–2; 1 COR 5:1–11; 2 COR 2:5–8

He made a mistake of which he was truly sorry. He knew he should not have but chose to any way. The consequences of his actions brought painful results. He had strayed away from the "pack" and was attacked by that hungry lion, the devil, who had sought him as his prey. Attacked and regretfully sorry for straying, he cried out to Jesus to deliver him from the jaws of this devourer. Jesus came and rescued him from the devil's clutches. Now he limps back to the pack seeking restoration and healing.

THE PACK'S RESPONSE

As he approached the "pack," they all gasped at the sight of his hideous wounds. A low bustle of hushed voices could be heard throughout the "pack." With tears in his eyes, he relayed that he was sorry for leaving the pack and for the awful things he had said to them when he left. "Had it not been for Jesus the devil would have devoured me for sure," he said. As he continued to approach the "pack," they began to back away from him, repulsed by his gaping wounds. "Will you help me?" he said.

A voice from the "pack" said, "You're getting what you deserve."

Another voice said, "It's not our problem, but yours."

"We told you so!" yet another voice declared.

"You made your bed now lie in it," said another.

"I know, I know," he said. "I should have listened, but I was arrogant and prideful and I am sorry for shunning you. I will carry these awful scars the rest of my life. Oh how I wish I would have listened." With that, true tears of regret began to flow down his face. "Will you forgive me? I truly am sorry."

> Dear brothers and sisters, if another believer is overcome by some sin, you who are godly should gently and humbly help that person back onto the right path. And be careful not to fall into the same temptation yourself.
>
> Gal 6:1 (NLT)

Our Response Should Be...

When a brother or sister in Christ has sinned and they are repentant, then we who are not caught up in sin should forgive and help them back on the path of faith and healing. However, I must make it clear that unless one is repentant of their sin they cannot be restored. Do you realize that in the case of those who will not repent, but continue in sin and fellowship with us as though nothing is wrong, we are to, in some degree, shun them? *What?*

> It is actually reported that there is sexual immorality among you, and such sexual immorality as is not even named among the Gentiles—that a man has his father's wife! ²And

you are puffed up, and have not rather mourned, that he who has done this deed might be taken away from among you. ³For I indeed, as absent in body but present in spirit, have already judged (as though I were present) him who has so done this deed. ⁴In the name of our LORD Jesus Christ, when you are gathered together, along with my spirit, with the power of our LORD Jesus Christ, ⁵deliver such a one to Satan for the destruction of the flesh, that his spirit may be saved in the day of the LORD Jesus.

1 Cor 5:1–5 (NKJV)

Wow! Let me be clear, we are talking about one who will not repent and yet lives as though nothing is wrong with their sinfulness. However, you must balance this with what Paul wrote to the Corinthians in his second letter to them.

I am not overstating it when I say that the man who caused all the trouble hurt all of you more than he hurt me. ⁶Most of you opposed him, and that was punishment enough. ⁷Now, however, it is time to forgive and comfort him. Otherwise he may be overcome by discouragement. ⁸So I urge you now to reaffirm your love for him.

2 Cor 2:5–8 (NLT)

Therefore, once one sees that they cannot continue in sin and be accepted by God and they repent, we must restore them through love.

Our next time together, we will look at how love deals with sin. If one is repentant, are you wiling to forgive and restore them as Christ is? Do you hurl words of condemnation or pour in words of truth and love to the repentant one? I close with this.

An Ex-Convict Seeks The Lord

Many years ago, there was a young man who walked away from Christ and started running with the "wrong crowd." He ultimately found himself in prison. Once he was released from prison, he came to Church with his mother. He sat there through the service as scared as a cat in front of the dog pound with a hole in the fence. He came to the altar with Godly sorrow and repented before God. He began to make great strides to follow Christ. One day at church, I could tell he was still struggling with his past so I said to him, "Bill, if Christ has forgiven you for all you have done, then so do I. And if God doesn't hold it against you and has forgotten about it, then so do I."

Will you say the same to the repentant one?

How Does Love Deal with Sin?

1 John 4:8,16; Eph 4:12–16; 1 Cor 13:4–8;
John 3:16–21; Prov 3:34; James 4:6

Incorrect Statement

"God is a God of Love," is a famous quote that sounds spiritual and true but is *not* true at all.

What? I thought God was a God of love. If that were true then love would define God. Love does not define God; God defines love because God *is* love.

> He who does not love does not know God, for
> God is love.
>
> 1 John 4:8 (NKJV)

When we allow ourselves to take *our* definition of love to define how God responds to us, we get confused and somehow think that God is being unfair when He responds in love. It seems that many times our definition of love does not include confrontation of sin but somehow lets it slide or at best does not completely deal with it to eliminate all together.

Because of this definition of "love," sin is allowed to remain. Not only that, but those who in "true love" confront sin are rebuffed as being judgmental.

If you want a correct definition of how loves deals with sin you must look at how God deals with sin.

LOVE COVERS A MULTITUDE OF SIN BY CONFRONTING IT

Since God is love and love covers a multitude of sin, how does God do that? Does He simply sweep it under the carpet? No, God confronts sin head on because He knows what sin is and what it will do in your life. The reason that Jesus came to earth was to confront our sins.

The attitude of God when confronting us with our sins is straight forward, firm with compassion, and mercy. With a correct understanding of "love," we are to operate in love when confronting the sin of another. Love does not confront with judgment but knows that unless our sin is dealt with, judgment will come.

> Brethren, if anyone among you wanders from the truth, and someone turns him back, ²⁰let him know that he who turns a sinner from the error of his way will save a soul from death and cover a multitude of sins.
>
> James 5:19–20 (NKJV)

LOVE ALSO SEEKS TO RESTORE

Love seeks to bring one back to right standing and health not to drive further away.

> Brethren, if a man is overtaken in any trespass, you who are spiritual restore such a one in a spirit of gentleness, considering yourself lest you also be tempted.
>
> Gal 6:1 (NKJV)

LOVE SEEKS TO DEAL WITH SIN AND GET ON WITH LIFE.

> *For I will forgive their iniquity, and their sin I will remember no more."*
>
> Jer 31:34b (NKJV)

One of the problems in the "church" world has been when a person truly repents of their sins, "Christians" will not let them forget their previous shortcomings. If the person has truly repented, meaning they have confessed their sin and committed to stop doing it, and have asked Jesus to forgive them, they are forgiven.

> If we say that we have no sin, we deceive ourselves, and the truth is not in us. ⁹If we confess our sins, He is faithful and just to forgive us our sins and to cleanse us from all unrighteousness.
>
> 1 John 1:8–9 (NKJV)

LOVE SEEKS TO GROW YOU

> But, speaking the truth in love, may grow up in all things into Him who is the head—Christ—¹⁶from whom the whole body, joined and knit together by what every joint supplies, according

to the effective working by which every part
does its share, causes growth of the body for the
edifying of itself in love.

Eph 4:15–16 (NKJV)

FOUL!

Why do some rebuff or cry foul when confronted in love
about their wrongs and/or sins? I can tell you from personal
experience when confronted in my own life the bottom line
reason is *pride*! Pride is all about "self-preservation." From
pride's point of view when you admit that you are wrong,
you damage your self-esteem. Therein lies the problem,
"self" esteems itself greater than God.

> For thus says the High and Lofty One Who
> inhabits eternity, whose name is Holy: "I dwell
> in the high ad holy place, With him who has a
> contrite and humble spirit, To revive the spirit
> of the humble, And to revive the heart of the
> contrite ones.
>
> Isa 57:15 (NKJV)

If you are confronted about being wrong or about sin
how do you respond? Do you rebuff and cry foul or do you
receive it and repent? If you are crying foul then pride is in
control. If you are the doing the confronting, what is your
attitude? Is your attitude that of seeking the best for that
individual or somehow making yourself feel better?

Seek to know love better by seeking *who* God is. To show
love, seek how God shows love.

THE DEADLY VENOM OF DECEIT

REV 12:9; 2 COR 11:14–15;
JOHN 8:31–32,34–36; 16:13–14; GAL 6:7–8

A fisherman along the banks of a Florida river spotted a beautiful snake with red and yellow bands running from its head to its tail. Now the fisherman usually would not pick up a snake, but it was not aggressive at all. In fact, it seemed to be curiously friendly. The snake did not have any fangs, just small little teeth. The fisherman picked up the snake, and the snake was not startled or aggressive. The snake loosely wrapped itself around the fisherman's hand.

The fisherman was quite amused at how docile the snake was. He began to playfully tease the snake with a finger of the hand the snake was wrapped upon. The snake ever so slightly bit down on his finger, which felt like an uncomfortable tickle.

Amused, the fisherman got into his boat with the snake still wrapped around his hand, gnawing on his finger, and he headed down the river. Several hours later, some fishermen found the man lying in his boat dead.

THE OLD ADAGE SAYS...

"Red touch yellow will kill a fellow but red touch black is good for Jack." That is a saying to distinguish between a deadly coral snake and a scarlet king snake. A coral snake is a relative of the cobra family and is very poisonous. The venom of a coral snake can kill you. Yet the coral snake does not have the classic "fangs" that a Rattlesnake or other poisonous pit viper would have. A coral snake gnaws on its victim and as it is gnawing, it is secreting its deadly venom. Another trait that makes the coral snake so deadly is that it does not look dangerous. It is beautiful in color, slender and usually less than two feet long. It is not aggressive, for the most part a recluse and therefore very deceptive.

WHAT IS DECEIT?

Deceit or deception is a lie presented as the truth. To be deceived is when one acts upon the deceit (the lie) as the truth. The deceiver is the devil. In the Garden of Eden, the devil tempted Eve by presenting a lie as the truth. Eve believed the lie as being the truth and acted upon the deception, therefore, she was deceived.

> Now the serpent was more cunning than any beast of the field, which the LORD God had made. And he said to the woman, "Has God indeed said, 'You shall not eat of every tree of the garden'?" ²And the woman said to the serpent, "We may eat the fruit of the trees of the garden; ³but of the fruit of the tree which is in the midst of the garden, God has said, 'You shall not eat it, nor shall you touch it, lest you die.'" ⁴Then the serpent said to the woman, "You will not surely die. ⁵For God knows that in the day

you eat of it your eyes will be opened, and you will be like God, knowing good and evil." ⁶So when the woman saw that the tree was good for food, that it was pleasant to the eyes, and a tree desirable to make one wise, she took of its fruit and ate. She also gave to her husband with her, and he ate. ⁷Then the eyes of both of them were opened, and they knew that they were naked; and they sewed fig leaves together and made themselves coverings.

Gen 3:1–7 (NKJV)

THE SERPENT

The Bible calls the devil the serpent in the Garden of Eden. The devil is also called an angel of light, appearing to be good and trusting, yet full of deadly venom. His main role is to deceive and cause people to sin. He is not alone in his effort either, for he has legions of demons bidding his trade.

Now the Spirit expressly says that in latter times some will depart from the faith, giving heed to deceiving spirits and doctrines of demons, ²speaking lies in hypocrisy, having their own conscience seared with a hot iron,

1 Tim 4:1–2 (NKJV)

Whether you realize it or not, everyday the devil and his demons are offering you lies as truth. "It is ok if you do this because ... No one will know about this, so what harm will it do if ... Hey so and so is doing it so ... God wants you to be happy so go ahead and ... " And on and on it goes.

The Adamic nature is extremely prone to be deceived. In fact, the Adamic nature thrives on deception and would rather believe a lie than the truth.

For the time will come when they will not endure sound doctrine, but according to their own desires, because they have itching ears, they will heap up for themselves teachers; 4and they will turn their ears away from the truth, and be turned aside to fables.

2 Tim 4:3–4 (NKJV)

THE SPIRIT OF TRUTH

Only through the Word of God and the Holy Spirit can we truly know the truth. The truth sets us free from deception and the truth will guard us from deception. That is why it is so important to be a student of the Word. Equally important is that your relationship with Christ is fresh moment by moment. The Holy Spirit is the link between you and Christ. The Holy Spirit will guide you into all truth. All truth is settled in the Word of God, so the Holy Spirit will never tell you something that is against the Word of God.

Do not play with the devil's deception. It may appear harmless but "red and yellow will kill a fellow."

Then the serpent said to the woman, "You will not surely die."

Gen 3:4 (NKJV)

IS THE STANDARD TOO HIGH?

HEB 12:14; JOHN 8:31–36; ROM 6; ROM 7:5–8:14, 31–39; 1 COR 10:13; JAMES 1:13–15; 1 JOHN 1:9

> They have all turned aside, they have together become corrupt; There is none who does good, no, not one.
>
> Psa 14:3 (NKJV)

THE HEADLINES

The Headlines read, "Conservative Pastor Caught In Affair." Another Headline read, "Pastor Arrested for Embezzlement of Church Funds." Still yet another headline reads of a minister arrested for DUI. Another read "Local Pastor Arrested"—for solicitation of prostitution of one of the same sex. Is the standard too high in that no one can live up to God's expectations?

THE ANSWER IS SIMPLE

The answer is no, the standard is not too high. Okay, so is the standard something that only a few can achieve and rest of us just live with the fact that we will never achieve that level? I mean if a minister fails to live to that standard then what hope is there for the "common" Christian?

HOW CAN A CHRISTIAN LIVE UP TO THE STANDARD?

This is going to sound extremely simplistic yet that is exactly what it is. As a Christian, you simply choose to live the standard. Well, easier said than done, you may say. God did not set us up for failure in Christ, but victory.

One of the passages of Scriptures that I have listed is Romans 7:5 through Romans 8:14 and 8:31–39 as well as John 8:31–36. In those passages of Scripture, it shows that when we receive Christ into our lives He sets us free from sin and we are now free to obey Him. Before Christ, we did not have a choice; we could not obey because sin had us bound. Now that we are free from sin and have the Spirit dwelling within us, we are free to obey God. All we have to do is simply obey the promptings of the Holy Spirit guided by the Word of God.

TEMPTATIONS

But what about all those powerful temptations we face to disobey? I mean I have fallen more than once into temptations, doesn't that mean I've failed to live up to the "standard"? Yes, but when we do fail, we have a means of regaining our status by repenting and asking Jesus to forgive us. However, you don't have to give into temptations. We are free from sin and we have the power through the Spirit to simply obey. (See 1 Cor 10:13; James 1:13–15).

IT IS YOUR CHOICE

The standard is not too high, we have been set free by Christ and empowered by the Spirit to live up to the standard through simple obedience. When a minister or seemingly "strong" Christian falls into sin, it was not because of one choice, rather a culmination of many choices to disobey, which lead to their downfall.

CHRIST OUR STANDARD

Outside of Christ, we cannot live up to the standard of God because Christ was the only one that in flesh lived up to the standard that God set in His Law. The Law shows us our sins, but Christ did not sin so in the flesh, He defeated sin by living up to the complete standard set by the Law and through Him, we too defeat sin.

What are you going to chose to do, simply obey or fail? The choice is yours.

> I can do all things through Christ who strengthens me.
>
> Phil 4:13 (NKJV)

THE HEART OF TWO KINGS–
PART 1

1 SAM 15

Their mission was a success; they defeated their enemy and now feasted upon the spoils of victory. There was singing and dancing, tales of the battle and laughter throughout the camp. However, nearly drowned out by all this merriment was the bleating of sheep and lowing oxen in the background. King Saul was extremely popular with the people that day. In the midst of this merriment came word to the King that the prophet Samuel was coming. The King hurried out to meet him and the elders of Israel followed closely by.

THE CONFRONTATION

"Blessings upon you, O prophet of God! I have completed what God has told me to do through your word," proclaimed the King.

Samuel rebuffed the King, "then why do I hear sheep and oxen among the people?"

The King, caught off guard by this rebuttal replied,

"Well they were brought from the enemy's fields because the people wanted to bring them back to offering them as a sacrifice to the LORD ... I can assure you we brought back the very best for a sacrifice but we destroyed everything else just like God said to do."

HOW GOD SEES IT

In anger Samuel said, "Hush! I am going to tell you what God told me about this!"

"Please, tell me," Saul said with a look of shock and puzzlement on his face.

"When you were a nobody, God chose you, exalted you and made you the King over all the tribes of Israel. You had no power of your own but God selected you to lead and be the example for the people to follow. God specifically told you: destroy the enemy completely because of their vile treatment to the Children of Israel when they were coming up from Egypt. But instead you chose not to obey God in that you did not destroy everything of your enemy's like God said to do."

DEFENDING AND BLAMING

"That's not true!" defended Saul. "I destroyed the enemy, I brought back their King as a prisoner of war, but it was the people's fault for bringing back the livestock, not mine. So I have obeyed God, and we will honor God by sacrificing the enemy's livestock to Him."

GOD IS NOT IMPRESSED

"Do you think God is impressed with your sacrifices," countered Samuel. "To obey God is to be accepted by Him. Partial obedience is the same as disobedience even if you couple it with sacrifices. You have no right claim obedience when you have purposely, partially obeyed Him. What you have done is rebellious and is equal to witchcraft in God's eyes. Your unwillingness to completely obey God is the same as worshiping idols, of which the biggest idol in your life is yourself. This is the reason that today God has rejected you as being the King of Israel."

HALFHEARTED CONFESSION

The pressure was on King Saul because the elders were present at this confrontation between he and Samuel. Saul had to act fast if he was going to save face with the elders and the people.

"Okay, you are right," admitted King Saul. "I was afraid of what the people would think if I forbade them to take the livestock, so I let them. So I admit; I sinned. Now will you come with me to worship God before the people?"

"No I cannot," Samuel said firmly. "You have rejected obeying God and God has rejected you as being King over Israel."

POLITICAL PRESSURE

With that, the Prophet turned to leave. Saul looked around and saw all the elders of Israel looking at the scene with mixed expressions among them. Some looked shocked, some shook their heads, some were confused, some murmured among themselves. Saul knew his political power was at stake, and he needed Samuel to appear with him before the people to calm the situation down.

In an act of desperation, he lunged at the prophet walking away, grabbed the arm of the robe, and spun Samuel around towards him. As he did, it ripped the robe of the prophet. A look of regrettable shock came across the face of Saul.

Samuel looked at the rip and then into the face of King Saul and said: "Just as you have ripped my robe, God has ripped the kingdom from your hands and is giving it to someone He can trust to obey Him. God has said this and He does not lie."

DESPERATE NEGOTIATIONS

Saul, in a move to calm the situation, put his arm around the prophet and pulled himself up close to him. Saul looked around sheepishly at the elders standing their watching. Saul pleaded with Samuel in a hushed yet desperate voice. "Okay, I admit; I've sinned ... ok? I need you to come with me to the public worship service ... I need you to be there with me so the people will not cause uproar. If they do not see you there with me, they will start anarchy ... Please! I'm begging you to do this!"

Reluctantly, Samuel went with Saul to the public worship service. King Saul went through the religious and stoic motions of the worship service. The King made sure that the elders and the people saw the prophet standing there with him.

WHAT WAS THE SIN OF KING SAUL?

Why did the sin of King Saul disqualify him from being the King of Israel? What was in Saul's life that could be in your life that would cause a severing of your relationship with God? Why did God allow David to remain King when Saul was not? Does God play favorites? In our next devotional, we will look at King David's sins and his response when confronted by Nathan, the prophet.

WHOSE HEART DO YOU HAVE?

As you read these devotionals about these two Kings, I ask you to ask yourself, "Whose heart do I have, King Saul's or King David's?"

THE HEART OF TWO KINGS– PART 2

2 SAM 11, 12

His troops were out to battle, but he, the King, had stayed behind at the palace. He was at the apex of his life. His life was truly was a rags to riches story, a story of toil to triumph, struggle to success. God had put him on the throne of Israel. No enemy could stand before him or his armies. He had all the material possessions he could ever want; he had wives, fame, fortune, success, songs written about him, the fear of all his enemies and the respect of all his subjects. However, there was restlessness in King David's life.

A RESTLESS NIGHT

One night, David could not sleep so he went out on his balcony to get some fresh air. As he stood there, casually surveying his surroundings, some movement caught his attention. He looked in the direction of the motion and there at another house he saw a woman bathing in the moon lit night. This woman did not know anyone was watching, but David's eyes were glued upon her. She was a very, very beautiful woman and David liked what he saw.

The next day he sent his servants to investigate to find out what her name was. They reported that she was Bathsheba, the wife of Uriah. Uriah was one of David's soldiers and he was out on the battlefield miles away. David devised a scheme to get Bathsheba closer to him. He invited her to have dinner with him at the palace. He wined and dined her, not just that evening but for several evenings. Before long, they were involved in a lustful affair. This affair went on for some time. David was having the best of both worlds and nobody knew about it.

THE PLOT THICKENS

One day Bathsheba came to the King crying and broke the news to him that she was pregnant. O boy, the King had to think fast on how to cover up this scandal. His fast thinking led him to call Uriah home from the battle. King David knew that a man away at battle for several months would enjoy a night in the arms of his wife. So the plan was that Uriah would come home, he would have a night with his wife, and it would then appear that the child was Uriah's and this whole messy scandal would just go away.

UNEXPECTED TURN OF EVENTS

King David encountered an unexpected problem with Uriah; he was a faithful man and a man of integrity and principle. Uriah would not sleep with his wife knowing the other married warriors of Israel would not have the same pleasure. Therefore, he would not go home to his wife but slept with the servants at the King's palace.

The next evening the King invited Uriah to dinner and eventually got him drunk with wine. He took him outside and pointed him to his house. The King knew for sure that the drunken husband would surely throw all principle and integrity out the window and sleep with his wife that night.

The next morning however, Uriah was found once again, sleeping in the servant's quarters; he never did make it home that night.

THE DEATH SENTENCE

King David was furious that Uriah's morals and standards were threatening his plan to cover up his scandal. Therefore, he wrote a letter to his field general Joab. Effectively, the King told Joab to put Uriah at the hottest point of the battle. When Uriah was in trouble, Joab was to withdraw his support so that Uriah would die. David sealed that letter and gave it to Uriah to give to Joab. Uriah had no idea that he was carrying his own death sentence.

David's plan worked. Uriah was killed in battle, David took the now widowed Bathsheba to be his wife and voila, problem solved, scandal covered up.

THE PROPHET ENCOUNTER

One day, the prophet Nathan showed up at the King's Palace. David, still blinded by his sin, did not think much of Nathan's visit. Nathan began to tell the King a story, "King, there are two men in your kingdom and they live beside each other. One man is extremely rich and has all the livestock he could ever need. The other man is a very poor man and only has one female sheep. In fact, this poor man has raised this sheep from birth. It has become a family pet, it sleeps in the house with the family, and they feed it from their table. You would think that the sheep is actually a part of the family."

By now, King David was fully intrigued by Nathan's story and could relate. As a young shepherd boy, David himself had had a pet sheep. He understood the love and bond that had developed between the family and the sheep in Nathan's story.

A Sad Yet True Story

"One day," Nathan continued, "the rich neighbor had a traveling friend that stopped by unannounced. The rich man had to prepare a dinner for his friend, but he didn't want to use one from his livestock. So he stole the poor mans sheep, killed it, and served it as dinner for his traveling friend."

With that, King David jumped to his feet, his face boiling with anger, and proclaimed, "That's the most hideous, selfish thing I've ever heard of! That rich man had no compassion or concern for the poor man. My God! I cannot believe someone would do such a thing! As God lives, this man will be executed and all his possessions shall be given to the poor man for such hideous atrocities!"

Your Are The Man

With a burst of Godly indignation, Nathan pointed his finger at David and said, "You're that man!" This caught the King by surprise and cut to his heart.

Nathan continued as David's countenance reflected the indictment that Nathan was handing down from God.

"God brought you from the sheep fields of obscurity. He delivered you from the murderous plots of King Saul. He gave you everything that was Saul's; all his land, possessions, wives ... everything! God has given you great success, so that no enemy can stand before. He has given you the entire Kingdom of Israel and given you peace within your borders. And if that wasn't enough, God would have given you much more! You have profaned the name of the LORD by doing these evil acts, and because of this the enemies of God will scoff. You have committed adultery. You took that poor man's sheep to be yours. He loved his wife and you killed him for being a man of integrity."

DAVID'S RESPONSE

With a broken heart and bitter regret, King David fell with his face to the ground and cried out. "Oh, God! I have sinned against You and You alone. And I have done this evil in Your sight! You are just to do whatever You deem right against me!"

PROBING QUESTIONS

King David's sins carried the death penalty according to the Mosaic Law, so why then was King David not rejected for his sins and carried outside the city gates and executed?

The sin of King Saul was partial obedience, so why was King Saul rejected by God for his sins?

What was the difference? Does God play favorites? Is God unfair?

Whom do the prophets in both stories represent?

Which heart do you have? How can you tell which heart you have?

These questions will be answered in the next chapter.

THE HEART OF TWO KINGS–PART 3

1 SAM 10:1–13; 1 SAM 11; 1 SAM 13:1–15;
1 SAM 14:24–46; 1 SAM 15; 1 SAM 16:1–13;
2 SAM 11; 2 SAM 12:1–14; GAL 6:7–9; PSA 51

If you have read the first two parts of this devotional, you have seen two Kings, two sets of sins, two different responses, and two different outcomes. On the surface, it looks as though God has played favorites with King David. God not only allowed David to remain the King but to live as well. King David committed two sins, which according to the Mosaic Law, carried the death penalty.

THE LAW DEMANDED DEATH!

According the Law, which God Himself established, both adultery and murder carried a mandatory death penalty. King Saul's sin was partial obedience to an order from God. That order was to utterly destroy the enemy. Why was King Saul rejected and King David not? What can we learn from the heart of these two Kings?

DID GOD VIOLATE HIS OWN WORD?

God will not violate His Word. So how do we reconcile the fact that it appears He did when He allowed King David to live? First, God does not play favorites; for the issue is *not* with God but with the kings. The heart of King Saul was not repentant and the heart of King David was. So let us look at some of the circumstances and reactions that reveal to us the heart that God receives and the one He rejects.

KING SAUL

If you will read 1 Samuel 10 you will see the account of the day Saul was anointed to be the King of Israel. Two verses stand out to me in this account:

> So it was, when he had turned his back to go from Samuel, that God gave him another heart; and all those signs came to pass that day. ¹⁰When they came there to the hill, there was a group of prophets to meet him; then the Spirit of God came upon him, and he prophesied among them.
>
> 1 Sam 10:9–10 (NKJV)

God gave him another heart. Saul was a changed man that day but he chose *not* to remain changed.

GOD'S ADMONITION TO ALL

Look also at the admonition of Samuel to not only King Saul but to the entire nation of Israel.

> And do not turn aside; for then you would go after empty things which cannot profit or deliver, for they are nothing. ²²For the LORD will not forsake His people, for His great name's sake, because it has pleased the LORD to make you His people. ²⁴Only fear the LORD, and serve

Him in truth with all your heart; for consider what great things He has done for you. ²⁵But if you still do wickedly, you shall be swept away, both you and your king.

1 Sam 12:21–25 (NKJV)

REPLACING GOD

As you read chapters thirteen and fourteen, you will see that Saul's heart moves to being self-centered and not God centered. He was concerned about his image before the people and what *they* wanted him to be. He began to justify partial obedience as being equal to complete obedience. Justifying your compromises is the path that leads you away from God. This process is done so easily.

SO COMMON YOU CANNOT SEE IT

Follow the path of compromising and you come to a point as King Saul did, that is you cannot even see your sins that are in plain view for all to see. Saul's sins, represented by the sheep and oxen, were crying out, but King Saul did not notice. You can become so used to your compromises and sins that you do not even notice them among you.

King David did the same; he justified his compromises that lead to sin. Surely sleeping in the arms of another man's wife is a sin that is obvious to King David. Both kings had become "desensitized" to the convictions of their conscience. Do we not do the same thing? Do we not allow ourselves to justify our compromises, even if ever so slightly? We know we should not, yet just a little compromise is okay because we have not fully indulged.

DEFENSE OF SIN

King Saul convinced himself that partial obedience was the same as obedience. What we see is that God sees partial obedience equal to complete disobedience. When Samuel confronted Saul about his disobedience, the first thing Saul did was defend himself against the accusations. When Samuel produced more evidence of Saul's disobedience, Saul produced more evidence to defend himself. King Saul even "spiritualized" his disobedience by pointing out the fact that the sheep and oxen were going to be given as a sacrifice to God. Spiritualizing disobedience is something people still do today.

SAVING FACE OVER SAVING GRACE

Saul was more concerned about saving face than saving grace. Saul was emphatic about Samuel worshiping God with him to save face with the people. King Saul never confessed that he had sinned against God. The closest we see to a confession is mere words that he had sinned against Samuel. It appears that he simply said those words to use as leverage to have Samuel worship God with him before the people.

AGAINST GOD AND GOD ALONE

King David seemed safe and secure in his deception and scandalous cover up. However, when Nathan confronted him, we see a completely different response than that of Saul. David immediately confessed that he had sinned against God and God alone. He knew that he was guilty and offered *no* defense to the charges brought against him by God.

TRUE HEART OF REPENTANCE

David had a true heart of repentance, which completely admits the sin when confronted by God. A heart of repentance is truly sorry from the depths of the soul. It is deep sorrow for offending God. It's a heart that loves God and knows that sin has led them to betray that love for God.

A heart of repentance also understands that God is just in whatever punishment He gives.

WHOM DO THE PROPHETS REPRESENT?

In both stories, the prophets, Samuel and Nathan, represent the Holy Spirit. When we sin, the Holy Spirit confronts us just as the prophets confronted the Kings. What do you do when confronted by the Holy Spirit about your sins? Do you give excuses and defenses or admit and repent?

WHOSE HEART DO YOU HAVE?

If you have a heart like King Saul, it will lead you to be rejected by God. If you have a heart like King David, there is grace and mercy awaiting you. You will still have to reap consequences for your sins, because God said that we reap what we sow. Yet our sins will be forgiven and washed away in the blood of Jesus and God will receive us.

> For godly sorrow produces repentance leading to salvation, not to be regretted; but the sorrow of the world produces death.
>
> 2 Cor 7:10 (NKJV)